The Primary

Marble

Author D.K. Charley

DEDICATION

To the struggling youth of our society. You are not alone.

Author Notes

I have talked to people from many walks of life. This book is everyone's life experiences that I've met including my own, put in one story, The Primary Marble. The main character, Daniel, despite being in his twenties is still a young boy. He wants to be happy. I hope this story can help young adults find their happiness. I hope it can help parents bond more with their children. Readers will probably get different interpretation from the book. This is because life experiences shape who we are and therefore our perception.

Life is about choices and Daniel will need to make many of those choices, just like everyone else. What is the truth? What is your meaning of life? Is it to learn? Or is it simply to live and experience the many emotions and obstacles we face. Are you born with disadvantages or have you not taken all the advantages you have? These are questions you should ask yourself while reading this story.

People say, with power comes responsibility. Mankind has one of the greatest powers, the power to make choices. As long as we are breathing we can make choices. We just need to be responsible for the choices we make. Addicted to drugs, crime or women, we have choices. The greatest problems with choices are without some guidance, it's hard to make the right choices.

Last but not least the main character will feel as there is no hope. However, it is when he surrenders himself he finds peace. The profanity is left in because it tells the story for how it happens, "the real world". The biblical quotes were left in because it aided in the main characters guidance. I realize these two put together may offend some, but I believe if they belong anywhere, it is in a struggling young man's life. I hope this book can help someone. For others I hope if anything you are at least entertained.

No matter where you are in life, it can always change.

This story is about my friend Daniel and his primary marble. The young man was searching for a childhood place called Halisaseas. Like many of us he faced adversities but with every triumph came enlightenment. This book is based on actual events. The names have been changed to protect those involved in the story.

ACKNOWLEDGMENTS

I would like to give special thanks to the following juvenile correction intuitions and their staff. Roebuck, Mt. Meigs, Central Oklahoma Juvenile Department, Georgia Boot Camp for Youth, and Los Angeles Youth Services. Thanks to my editor, Peter Heyrman, my family and my higher power.

CHAPTER 1

The young Marine, Daniel, lay motionless. His past flashed before him in pictures, as gravity started to slip away. Unable to move, he felt the cool breeze and fresh air spiral around his lifeless body.

The thought occurred to him that he had died serving his country, but Daniel knew, "Marines aren't allowed to die without permission." At that moment the images faded away. He concentrated on one picture.

"You will be alright", said a gentle voice.

As he focused on the caramel complexion of a young girl's face, reality slowly emerged. As he gazed into her hazel eyes, she gave him an empathetic look. Her small soft hands took a hold of his.

Momentarily mystified by her beauty, he struggled to assess his situation. Sadness mixed with frustration of the unknown, overwhelming him. Snatching his hand from her soft fingers, he brushed against something like nylon. Tugging on one side of the fabric, the other side pulled violently against his wrist.

Daniel realized he was strapped down to a gurney. Cold fluid streamed through his veins. He checked himself for mobility, but it was useless. He could control only his eyes and three right fingers. Even these soon failed him. Grasping for the small object poking out of his right pocket, he surrendered to a deep sleep. As he lost consciousness, he wished he could return to a place called Halisaseas.

He awakened to the rumbling of the aircraft as it descended over the Pacific Ocean. The plane turned left and approached the edge of an island. As it flew over open plains, a landing zone appeared. Daniel was pleased to see the vibrant green grass. He couldn't wait to put his feet on the ground, but this was not Halisaseas.

The plane angry vibrating sound came to a stop. Daniel couldn't feel the landing, but he regained his sense of gravity. Two men, who appeared to be Navy corpsmen, dashed to the side of the aircraft, grabbed the gurney, and pulled him out.

Daniel was rushed into the hospital. He panicked as lights on the ceiling passed before his eyes. The gentle voice was nowhere to be found. He was pushed into a place similar to an operating room, yet different. There were no forceps, no scalpels or medical devices.

"The Doctor will be with you shortly," the corpsmen said.

As Daniel waited, he tried to recall the incidents that led up to here. Suddenly, he remembered arguing with his superior officers, and an explosion. He knew he was in serious trouble. He tried to remain calm as the Doctor entered the room.

"How are you?" the Doctor asked.

"I'm fine sir, but what's going on?" Daniel replied.

Bending over Daniel, the gray-haired Colonel examined him. "You're okay; you've been through a lot."

Daniel shook his head in agreement.

"You passed out from extreme dehydration and hit your head," the Doctor said. Daniel thought how disappointed he was from the absence of blood. "No blood, No honor" Daniel mumbled.

"I have to take a piss sir" Daniel said to the Doctor, as if he was talking to his grandpa. Grandpa could never say no. The Doctor responded, "Just one minute," then flashed a light in his eyes. He began asking Daniel questions.

"Is your head okay?"

"Yes."

"Do you feel when I push here?"

"Yes"

"I'm going to release you and sit you up. Is that okay?"

"No, Doc. I'd rather lay here and piss on myself if you don't mind," Daniel responded in a groggy attempt at wit.

The Doctor gave Daniel a half grin and took off the restraints.

"In Halisaseas there are no restraints, mentally or physically," Daniel said in a low voice.

"What's that?" the Doctor asked.

"Nothing sir," he responded.

The Doctor performed a few more procedures, checking Daniel's legs and arms. He asked Daniel to bend over so he could check his spine. "I'm relieved to see everything is working well," the Doctor said. The Navy corpsman came back in, and escorted Daniel to the bathroom. Daniel noticed every door had a lock. Craving optimism, he hoped this was a precaution to keep the enemies out. As he and the corpsman walked together, Daniel wondered if he could just leave.

As they reached the bathroom door, the corpsman said, "Go into the head and disrobe."

"Can I piss" Daniel asked.

The young Navy man looked at him and responded, "Yes, then put this on."

He handed Daniel a pair of blue faded scrubs and a hospital gown. Without thinking, Daniel rushed into the head to relieve himself. Finishing, he turned, and noticed the blue scrubs and thin top that he'd dropped on the floor. He stopped and looked at them. He recalled receiving a similar wardrobe at the age of thirteen. This was patient's garb. As he put on the scrubs and top, he realized he wasn't going anywhere. He was a patient.

Walking out into the hall, Daniel was ordered to throw his uniform and personal effects into a bag.

"Can I keep this?" he asked, holding a marble in his right palm.

"No, everything has to go in the bag, the corpsman said.

Daniel slowly dropped the marble along with his pocket Bible and blue citizen watch into the trash bag.

"You can keep this," the corpsman said, handing him back his Bible.

Daniel responded dully, "I don't think I need this anymore," and dropped the Bible back in the bag.

The corpsman escorted Daniel through many doors; they all seemed the same, locked. They walked into a huge room with a lot of windows. It resembled a waiting room. Scratches on the glass windows looked like evidence of penned-up animals trying to escape. All of the windows had iron bars on the outside. The walls were covered in green and blue squares.

Before Daniel could speak up in protest, the scrawny corpsman shoved him into another empty room, smaller than the other. "Wait here," he said.

Daniel turned around and saw blue gym mats padding the walls and the floor. "This is a fucking asylum!" he screamed. He slid down to the floor and placed his knees in his chest trying to control his breathing. "I'm losing my military bearing," Daniel whimpered.

Daniel's heart started to hurt; his breathing got harder; he struggled to inhale. He put his hands on his chest. He exhaled. As his breathing accelerated, a sharp pain shot through his body. If this was a nightmare, maybe he could dream of another place.

Trying to regain his composure, Daniel imagined walking through the woods. He pictured an exhausted man trying to navigate a rugged path. The man stumbled over stumps and abandon logs, looking for a forgotten place. The man fell and seemed to give up. "Hush," he whispered to Daniel. "Be still. Get your bearings. Focus on the mission. I am Aadil. I will help you find this place you seek, but first we must journey from whence you came."

A sudden chill brought Daniel back to reality. He wondered if he had made the right decisions. He could not recall the events that led to his near insanity. He just wanted to serve his four years, go home, and have a family. But this dream seemed more and more distant. He'd never really felt like a ladies man. He was dark, short, and well-muscled, but was extremely shy around women.

Daniel wondered why the world picked on him. *Do they all deserve to die?*

he asked himself. Tears fell from his eyes like raindrops. He grew frantic. He had no one to call, no one to talk to.

Most Marines are prepared to die, but are trained not to. As he performed his duties, Daniel blocked out his past life to avoid distractions. Marines do whatever it takes to accomplish the objective. Marines protect the innocent. It's about defending the oppressed and protecting a way of life.

"Defend the poor and fatherless;

Do justice to the afflicted and needy.

Deliver the poor and needy;

free *them* from the hand of the wicked."

PSALMS 82: 3-4

In his heart Daniel had always wanted to help the oppressed, so all of this came naturally, but now he was the one who felt oppressed. Daniel only knew one way out: Kill everything!

He gathered all the disciplines he'd learned, and compared his present experience with the hardships he'd endured before. He suddenly realized: "This isn't anything." Then he waited. Hours seemed to pass. He heard the door unlock. When the door opened, a civilian nurse entered, and escorted him out to the waiting room. The nurse had the same questions the Doctor had asked. Daniel wanted something to eat, but he thought asking would be a sign of weakness.

After the intake processing, they gave him two sheets, and led him to an open bay. Beds were lined up in uniform rows. Though tired and hungry, he made up his bunk to military standards, folding the top sheet to form a 45-degree angle. When he was finished, Daniel looked around and saw eight other men sleeping in the room.

Instead of sleeping, Daniel lay down at attention, and waited for one of the others to attack him.

Hours later he heard footsteps in the hallway. The door opened, and someone shouted: "Chow time in ten minutes." Daniel sat up. He smoothed the wrinkles from his sheets, and thought: "Perfection." He got a small satisfaction from this effort. Lingering, he waited to see what the other patients would do. When they went into the lobby, he followed. There they sat and waited. Others arrived, and within a few minutes the area began to get crowded. Five girls walked into the room.

Daniel watched and observed. The room had a sad ambiance. The men formed up single-file in front of a gated door to the hallway, then marched to the cafeteria. Daniel searched for escape routes, but found none. They were served typical hospital fare, not like the food in the base cafeteria. The base had a section for pizza and pasta, and another line for beef, along with a salad bar and dessert selection. Here in the hospital all they got were fruit and cereal.

Daniel watched one of the girls cut the corner of a banana with her fork, and put it in her mouth. She put the fork down in disgust, and said she had to go to the latrine. "An Army girl", he said to himself, noting her army vernacular, "and bulimic at that. I wonder if she would have been opposed to eating some of my meat." The thought was his attempt to find humor in his situation.

The girl's request to go to the latrine was denied. Daniel suddenly pictured her throwing up on his penis, and all sexual thoughts of her faded. He knew it was bad to fantasize about this redheaded Irish girl with her perky breasts, but convicts and Marines have only one of two things on their minds: fighting or fucking, Daniel tried to think only of fighting.

The conversation at his table was about the girl. "How messed up these guys are, talking about her," he thought, then he noticed it was just one guy talking to himself. The guy was saying how crazy she was. The Irish girl started to cry. Breakfast ended. They marched back to the ward, and remained there, waiting for further instructions. They had books, but no TV. As each man was called back to an office, Daniel was ready to leave, whatever it took.

His name was soon called: "PFC Daniel Black."

"Sir! Yes, sir!" He stood up and headed to the office. There he found the old Colonel he'd met when he'd arrived.

The Doctor asked him: "Is there anyone to notify?"

"No! Can I please have my marble?" Daniel demanded.

"What marble?" the Doctor responded.

"The marble I came in with, sir!" Daniel said

"I will look into it. Is there anything else you need?"

"I just want to leave," said Daniel.

The Colonel told him he would be okay, and said he would try to get him out soon as possible. He handed Daniel a stack of papers and told him to go back into the waiting room. Daniel stood at attention, took one step back, and performed an about face. Sitting in the waiting room he glanced over the documents. They said he'd been admitted to the hospital for mental illnesses.

Many of the patients played ping-pong. Others rocked, or paced back and forth, and one pissed himself. Daniel picked up a book. He started reading about the disorders listed in his file. Glancing over he noticed several lacerations on one of the girl's arms. "She didn't do it right," he thought. He wanted to ask her why she was trying to kill herself. He could've instructed her on the proper way to do it; then she could stop suffering. Listening to other patients talk about their situations, he began to feel pathetic. He felt like giving up, just like the girl trying to commit suicide. Now his fellow Marines would fight in Iraqi Freedom without him.

Every day Daniel studied one of his new disorders. According to his file he was bipolar, antisocial, homicidal, suicidal, and had a personality disorder, with moderate delusions. That evening a nurse came in and called everyone one by name. They had to take their medication. Just as Daniel felt glad that he was not on medication, the nurse called him up.

"Do I have to take medication?" he asked.

"Yes," said the nurse. "If you don't we will have to put it in your arm, and you will never go home."

Daniel held three horse-sized pills in his hand. "Whatever it takes," he thought, putting the pills in his mouth. The nurse checked his mouth and instructed him to return to his seat. Time seemed to speed up. He would take his medication and read every day.

Something like a week passed before he next saw the Colonel. He was still "PFC Daniel Black," just as before.

"I had a look at your file," said the Doctor. "Now, Daniel, I want you to tell me everything you can remember from the beginning".

"Can I have my marble?" Daniel snapped.

"If I give you the marble will you tell me everything?" the Doctor asked.

Confused by this tactic, Daniel answered: "Yes."

The Doctor opened a small drawer on the right side of his desk, and rolled what appeared to be a red and yellow marble toward Daniel.

Daniel caught it, and began an analysis to confirm that this was his. As he ran his fingertip over its surface he felt the chipped place from his childhood. Suddenly the marble regained its primary colors. "There's the blue," Daniel thought. He looked up to see if the Doctor noticed, but there was no reaction. Satisfied Daniel continued, "You want me to start when I joined the military?"

"No," said the Doctor. "I want to know you. Start with your childhood, and that marble."

Daniel began with "The Primary Marble."

CHAPTER 2

Here is what Daniel said:

To understand this marble, sir, you must first understand me. I was born in Mobile, Alabama on August 20th,1982. I can remember when I was seven years old, looking out the amber, diamond-shaped window of our front door. As the sun set over the old, two-story brick house my grandmother had left our family, the sky faded. I waited and waited by the front door for a man I never met. I paced around the house until my mother barked: "Sit down, Daniel!"

As she got up from the couch, and walked up the stairs, each step telegraphed her anger. Then the door upstairs slammed. My entire body shook. I knowing something was wrong but I didn't know what. I went to the steps to listen, and then looked through the stained-glass window on the side of the front door. I glanced back at the stairs.

I could only hear half of the conversation, but I knew my wait was over. "Don't worry about it!" she shouted. I heard the phone receiver slam into its cradle, and knew my mother was upset. This was nothing new. She always looked unhappy. At seven years of age I didn't understand a lot, but I knew I was not going to be happy that day. In what seemed like a few minutes, I heard softer footsteps coming my way. There was a soft thump, as if a door were releasing frustration as she closed it. Once I was sure it was my mother, I hurried back to the couch in the foyer, acting as if I'd been there the entire time.

"Go into the living room, take off your shoes, and watch TV," she told me.

Thinking I had done something wrong. I bowed my head in shame and started to cry. "Why was I even born?" I mumbled. "Is she my real mom?" I asked myself, thinking I might have been kidnapped from my real family. My mom never treated me like she loved me or what I thought love was.

I trudged into the living room, continuing to cry. My cousin Pam, an overweight five-year-old with bumps on her face, and her hefty 9-year old brother, Terrance, just looked at me. I could only guess what they were thinking behind those twisted smiles. Hearing them chuckle made me feel like I didn't belong, I cried harder and louder. Suddenly a dull pain shot through the side of my face. I got up, noticed a shoe, and sat back down. My mother had just thrown that shoe at me.

"Shut up," she said, so I did.

As my cousins laughed at my humiliation, I sulked. I waited for my mother to leave. As she cast her face down, and walked away, I couldn't tell if she felt remorse or embarrassment. I stood back up. When no one was watching, I darted for the door. Outside I headed for the woods.

Terrance had told me stories of strange happenings in those woods. My mom had forbidden me to go there because of the snakes. As I fled into the woods I kept crying. It started to sprinkle. I took shelter beneath a tall fig tree, sat Indian-style, and started playing with the leaves. Tears trickled down my face. I kept my head down, covering my face with my hands. Light pierced my fingers. Looking up through the mist, I saw a rainbow. Standing, I stared at the beautiful colors. Animals played all around me.

A voice reassured me: "Daniel it will be okay." I tiptoed towards the voice, leaves crunching under my bare feet. As I got closer the rainbow started to fade. So did the rain. The sun lit my path. The rainbow vanished. I saw I was alone. When my last tear fell, I wiped my face with the back of my sleeve. A gray-and-white squirrel swooped down and landed in front of me.

"So you saw a flying squirrel?" the Doctor interjected, giggling.

"I guess. Can I continue?" Daniel asked, irritated by the Doctor's condescending tone.

"Yes," the Doctor replied. "Go ahead, Daniel."

I had always seen white squirrels outside the tree line, and I had always wanted to catch one. This one, standing just a few feet away from me, seemed different. It appeared to be happy, fearless and free to go wherever it wanted. I looked at it sadly. I wanted to be just like this squirrel.

"If I were a squirrel, where would I go?" I asked myself.

As the squirrel came closer, I saw it had something in its paws. The squirrel dropped the thing, and scurried up a tree. I looked to see what it was. I bent down, and picked it up. As I wiped away the mud, I saw that I had a red, yellow and blue marble.

Suddenly I got distracted by a boy who looked just like me, but he was happy. He stood naked and shameless. "I know the place you are searching for," he said. "And I will guide you, Daniel." I had no idea what he meant, but it sounded better than going home. He turned, and walked away; I followed. As we walked I told him how unhappy I was. He assured me the place where we were going was full of happiness and love.

"Watch out for the snakes," he said. "Some may look bright and beautiful, some white and pure, but they are very dangerous. They blend in with the surroundings. If you get too close you'll get bitten, so stay on the path."

We walked for what seemed a long time. I was getting hungry and tired. A hissing sounded from a bush. I saw a beautiful serpent, just as the boy had warned me. I turned to tell my friend, but he was no longer there. I heard the screaming: "Daniel, Daniel, come on." I was no longer afraid of the lioness paws of my mother.

I ran away from the snake towards the screaming. Finally I reached the house. As I came in through the back door somebody shouted, "There he is! There!"

I stood in the doorway. My mother rushed into the living room yelling, "Get in the corner!"

The Doctor interrupted Daniel: "Did you tell your mom about the naked boy in the woods and the snake?"

"No. She never listened," Daniel replied.

The Doctor shook his head in disbelief, and motioned for Daniel to continue.

While I stood in the corner, I asked if I could go pee-pee. Receiving no answer, eventually I peed on myself. My mom whipped me with three switches braided together. I ran up the stairs trying to escape. I darted under, then out from the bed. I tried the closet, but finally my little cousin, Dustin, held me down for her.

My mother always beat me out of anger. She would go until she couldn't swing anymore, or until I stopped screaming because I was too numb to hurt. After getting beaten with switches, I always had to take a bath that reeked of rubbing alcohol. The smell made me dizzy, and the pain burned my wounds. I sat in the bathtub, and knew my mother was being told not to beat me until she calmed down. She never took that advice. Pam was never beaten; nor was Terrance, at least not that I know of.

I made friends with a boy across the street named Q, but never really hung out with others due to my mother. Q and I could fight, yet be friends the next day. Even when we were kicking at each other's necks, and punching each other in the chest, it wasn't out of anger. It was out of respect.

Our friendship ended because people told my mother Q was bad news. In truth, I was the troublemaker. I was jealous of most kids. On hot summer days in Alabama, while other kids played, I was stuck on the living room couch, or I was cleaning. In an attempt to be fair, my mother sometimes let me stay out until the streetlights came on. But there was more to it than that.

I think the family was starting to complain about my obsessive weight gain. At one point my mother gave me the liberty to stay outside. She wouldn't let me come in from sunrise until the streetlights came on that evening. I had to eat and pee outside. One day it was so hot, that Pam and I cooked an egg on the black tar road in front of our house.

One calm, muggy Fourth of July my cousins played with fireworks on the side of the house. As my mother got ready for a party, she forbade me to play with them. I couldn't resist. I found a firecracker—a cherry bomb, I think—on the ground. When I picked it up the stem was hanging off. I tried to push it back in. My cousins threw firecrackers at me.

I ran in the house, grabbed my Uncle's lighter, ran back out, and got behind Terrance. I lit the stem—nothing. As Terrance turned to laugh—Bang! It exploded in my hand. As everyone started to laugh, I saw my skin was pulled back, exposing the white meat. Patches of my fingers and palm were black and wet. My hand throbbed, but I didn't cry. I wanted to, but I didn't. I wrapped my hand up in my shirt and slowly walked into the house.

My cousins followed me, still taunting. When they told my mother she screamed at me, and made me stay inside. My Aunt Ruby came from the back room and looked at my hand. She told my mother that I needed to go to the hospital. Instead my mother kept screaming that I would have to stay in the corner for the rest of the night. I played with my marble until she left. Whenever I played with my marble nothing around me bothered me. My mother finally went to the party with some of her friends.

My Aunt Ruby and Big Dustin were supposed to watch me, but as the eggnog set in they made other plans. They went back to the room where they put on a dirty movie. Then they did what married people do behind closed doors. I could hear the moans over the cheesy music. Soon I was outside shooting firecrackers across the street at neighbors and friends. It was as if we were at war. When a couple of bottle rockets whistled past my head, I decided to call it a night. I went back in to the couch.

Before the sun came up I saw more than a seven-year-old should see. Around 2 am I heard noises in the bathroom. I lay down on the couch for about a minute, waiting for the noise to stop. A little while later I had to use the toilet. I walked to the door and knocked. No answer. I could tell the only light in the bathroom came from the nightlight by the sink.

I was sure I heard noises, but I really had to pee. I turned the handle slowly. As I edged the door open, my eyes adjusted, and I couldn't turn away. I stared at her face. She was beautiful. With long curly hair falling below her shoulders, her eyes hypnotized me. Her lips were full, and her face was as beautiful as the rest of her body. Totally naked, she had a leg on the sink. I looked at her breasts then my eyes went to the hand she held between her legs. She was splashing water between her thighs. The lady grinned, and whispered, "Hello." I shut the door and hurried back to the couch.

I lay on the couch, wondering who she was. I heard her go to my uncle's room. "Why would anybody be attracted to Bill?" I asked myself. He was extremely fat, and wore a jheri curl. Was it because he drove a Porsche? Or because he had a post office job with benefits?

He'd gone out earlier that night, wearing a 1970s-style neon green suit. He brought home a girl half his age. I began fantasizing. What if I'd just asked for a feel? Then I realized I still had the urge to relieve myself. I returned to the bathroom, opened the door, and found a wet floor. I stood in front of the toilet and went.

Sometime later that morning I would see Aunt Ruby running naked from her room to the bathroom. Bill would take his girlfriend home. As she left she glanced at me on the couch and smiled. "Thank you, too, ma'am," I breathed, as I peeked from beneath the covers, and saw her go out the front door.

My mother returned early that morning and took me upstairs to bed. As she patted me to sleep, it was the most love I had felt from her in a long time. I slept all day long; so did she.

Things returned to normal after that. There was no party for my 8th birthday, just a card. Days of yelling and beatings started up again as soon as I got bad grades. My mother was embarrassed. She couldn't do things for me that other parents did for their kids. If she could've just said what she really felt, instead of letting me think she didn't love me, things might've been better. As a child all I could see was what my cousins got, and the way they were treated. When they told their mother something, she believed them. I saw this trust as love. I thought of gifts and quality time as love, like when Pam's mother gave her a huge party for her birthday, or when Terrance's stepfather took him fishing. I had no one—no love.

CHAPTER 3

That year my feeling of not belonging grew. All my cousins had their fathers and mothers with them. When I turned nine it seemed like every adult in the house wanted to raise me. There were my Uncle Bill, my Uncle Carson, my Aunt Ruby, and Grandpa Pat. Uncle Dustin was there, as were Little Dustin, and Brandy. My mother didn't mind the help. Her mother had abandoned her, and fled to California.

My aunts and uncles believed in raising a man to support his family and go to church on a regular basis. On the other hand, my grandmother, a Muslim, didn't approve of my mother's belief in Jesus Christ. My grandmother hadn't liked my father, so she disapproved of me. For a while it seemed like no one loved me, and I wondered why. Every day I did chores from sunup to sundown. I knew I was a bastard child; that's how I was treated.

One day a GT Mustang convertible pulled up in front of our house. It was sky blue with sprinkles and white leather seats. A man stepped out and briefly spoke to my mother. Though I could see that she knew him, she didn't approve of him. He motioned for me. I hesitated. My mother said to go with him. I slowly walked around the car to the passenger side. I gave my cousins a malicious smile, and pulled the door handle. I opened the door and got in.

We drove off, leaving my mother, and everyone else behind. For about ten minutes the man said nothing. Finally he asked: "Are you hungry?"

"Yes, sir," I said, rocking back and forth with excitement.

"What would you like to eat?"

I looked up at him. "Are you my dad?"

"Yes," he said, pulling into a fast food restaurant. He told me to order whatever I wanted.

I was so excited he had to order for me. The burger I got was huge, and the fries were overwhelming. Chili and cheese topped everything.

He took me to his mother's house. A lot of men were gathered on the porch. They all knew me, but I didn't know any of them. I walked to the room where I would meet his Mother.

"This is your grandmother," he said.

She stretched her arms out for me and I ran into them. I saw there was a lot of love here, and I didn't care where it was coming from. It was something I wanted and needed. For the next two days I didn't see my father. It didn't bother me. I ate whatever and whenever I wanted, and went to sleep anytime I liked.

My dad showed up and spent a couple of hours with me. He'd just missed my ninth birthday, so he let me pick out any gold necklace I wanted from his collection. He had all kinds of necklaces. Most of them were way too big for me, so I settled for one with a cross on it. He told me to get my things together and meet him at the car. We were going back to my mother's. I was sad to go back, but I knew I had no choice. I'd barely had a chance to get to know him.

When we got to my mother's he gave her a huge box of used toys. Lifting the box from the trunk, he said the toys were for me. I'd had such a great time that I'd forgotten about all the slave work I was coming back to. Inside I opened the box of toys, but my cousins pulled me away from it. Those toys were the only things I had from my father. I started swinging my fists. My aunts and uncles stopped me. They sat me down in the corner, and made me watch my cousins play with my toys. My mother said they were teaching me to share. That would've been okay, but my cousins never shared their stuff with me. Everyone always told me to keep my hands off things that didn't belong to me. As always, I was confused.

I was always confused, but I only got a beating if I asked for clarification. Doing that was the same as "talking back." But as my cousins tore my box apart, anger boiled up inside me.

I sat in the corner and stared through their souls. They kept antagonizing me. I began staring at the axe by the back door, when a beautiful marble rolled from the cluster of toys. I picked it up. I was astonished. It was my marble. How did it get there? Did I accidentally drop it in there? I didn't even remember having it. As I looked at the marble I swore to myself it would be the one thing no one would ever take from me. I rolled it trough my fingers, thinking: *One day we will be far away from here.*

Three more marbles spilled from the broken box. I scrambled over, and grabbed them off the floor. Back in my corner, I began playing a game. I lined up three marbles. "Look Pam," I said to my cousin, "this is you too." I rolled them around. Three times my marble bounced off the others, and came back to me. The fourth time it rolled under the couch. When I retrieved it the blue and yellow had disappeared, and what was left was blood red. I was staring at this new color when Pam got up and snatched the marble from me. I sunk my teeth deep in her arm. Blood welled up from her broken skin.

"Ruby!" She screamed to my aunt. "Daniel got out of the corner and bit me!"

With that, they had to go home. As Pam left, she grabbed the other three marbles.

I had to hold the table and bend over. All the adults started going on about how bad I was. They said biting was disgusting, and that I was a dog. Meanwhile Ruby beat me with my granddaddy's cane, and told me never to touch girls. I clutched the one marble in my right hand—my primary marble. I smiled. My mother was crying.

Beatings were my way of life. Sometimes my mother would beat me just to make herself feel better. Once, she left me at the house with some adults, saying she would be right back. She didn't come back for two days. When she finally returned, I cried and asked where she'd been. She started beating me with a pot. I knew she was wrong because the only thing the others would do was say: "You're not supposed to ask adults where they've been."

After that my mother wanted to raise me alone, so she decided to move out of the house. She knew she had to take better care of my sister and me. She was pregnant. We moved into the projects of Mobile. Though I have only cloudy memories of this, I know I got accustomed to street life.

"What do you mean by 'street life'?" the Doctor asked.

Daniel looked at him and said, "Poverty, sir."

Within a year my mother married my father's best friend, then divorced him. Though we had a couple of cold, hungry nights, my new sister, Adrian, and Mother, and I were together. The man my mother had married was named Cedrick. Cedrick was a skinny, dark-skinned fellow. He never had a real job, and everyone said he was a hustler. He made money taking any odd jobs he could find. He would work on cars, sell drugs, or cut grass. Their marriage lasted until my mother decided that she wanted to wear the pants. In all her relationships with men, she wanted to be the boss.

She argued with Cedrick, and screamed in his face, shrieking: "Slap me! I dare you! SLAP ME!" Ruefully Cedrick obliged.

Finally she divorced him. They didn't work anything out; they just got a divorce. Cedrick's sons from another woman left with him, and forgot all about me. We were alone again.

The only place we could afford was a tiny apartment in Prichard Projects. At night we heard sounds of people getting raped, tortured, and even murdered. I had nightmares about dying. I was always afraid.

"You know the dreams where it seems like you're falling?" Daniel asked the Doctor.

He smiled, and nodded in agreement.

"Well, I had them up until I was eleven, then it turned into me being shot."

At night the sounds were horrible. I asked my mom: "If God loves us why do we have to die?"   "That's not God's work," she said. "It's the work of the Devil. The Devil is like a snake. He tricks people into stealing and killing." Her words reminded me of my friend in the woods who'd warned me about snakes. We all slept on the floor just in case bullets came through the windows. It was our nightly routine.

When we gathered in the kitchen to celebrate my tenth birthday, I got a cupcake, and that was it. That's about the time my mother decided to start over. Once again she turned to the family. We returned to the place we called the "Big House," where my uncles and aunts lived. Once we got back there I took on a new attitude. All the time we'd been gone my mother had urged me to voice my opinion, and to talk to her about things. "It's only us," she would say. When I was 10 I witnessed my drunken Uncle Andrew get into my 27 year old mom's face. He said she'd never be shit. He shouted that no man would want her, and called her a slut.

She cried so hard. I gripped my primary marble. For the second time it turned red, and I thought about killing someone. He got right in my mother's face, yelling, and pushing her.

I hated Uncle Andrew. Whenever his wife, Pam's mother, cooked up her delicious soul food, I would head to their house (a trailer next to the Big House) for a plate. But whenever he was there, as soon as I walked in the door he would hit me. "Pull up your pants!" he would yell. I would try, but he was so old-fashioned that he wouldn't have been satisfied until I got them up to my chest. So now I started doing what I wanted to do, accepting whatever consequences came.

My cousins in Alabama were just as messed up as everyone else, but they thought they were different from those up North. My cousins from Ohio also tried to rebel when they visited. At one family reunion my cousin, Barbara, an older girl, went into Little Dustin's room. (He was also my cousin.) More cousins and I went to the room across the hall, where we were having fun jumping from the second floor patio porch to the ground.

About fifteen minutes had passed. Thinking Little Dustin was gone, I wanted to show my Ohio cousins his BB gun collection, which he'd mounted on the wall. When I peeked in the door it was just like in the movies. What appeared to be two people moving under the covers, their heads at the foot of the bed facing my way. Dustin yelled "Close the damn door!"

I didn't think much about it at the time. What had I seen? Was it Barbara and 19 year old Little Dustin? My mother had taught me that if a person knows better, but does something anyway, he or she will be judged for their sins. Even I knew what they were doing was wrong.

The family in the South preached a lot but never practiced what they preached "Do as I say, not as I do," they would tell me. Then they would leave us all night to go gambling in Mississippi. They knew what the Bible said about money. They'd heard the preacher tell them on Sunday mornings:

"Whoever loves money never has money enough;

Whoever loves wealth is never satisfied with his income.

This too is meaningless." (Ecclesiastes 5:10)

The Doctor said: "So how did that make you feel?

Daniel responded: "Like they wanted me to be something they couldn't be."

The chores got so bad, that my cousins from Ohio would run away every time they visited. I remember my 17-year-old cousin, Sydney and his family visiting the south from Ohio. The family tried to tell him to cut the grass and things like that. He didn't live there, so he refused and ran away. He escaped to a local restaurant and called the police. The police brought him back to the Big House. After the officers left, he argued with my Uncle Bill, Andrew and a few others. His mother watched as they verbally abused him.

He turned to her and said, "Fuck you. How can you stand there and watch this. You're not acting like my mother."

They beat him until blood ran down the side of his face, painting the grass a dark red. As he rolled over the grass stuck to his hands. He took repeated kicks to the abdomen. Nobody helped him. I was too young.

I hated the South after that and I think my mother started to dislike it too, but she was afraid. Maybe she thought that life couldn't change, but I knew in my heart that there was a better place. There was so much gossip there; people only cared about themselves. Though they pretended to be different from the family up North, they argued about any and everything. Then they'd go to work and gossip some more. They gossiped about everything, even calling each other from work just to talk about *The Young and the Restless* or *Days of Our Lives*.

"Paul cautions widows against entertaining the habit of gossip and of being idle. These women are described as 'gossips and busybodies, saying things they ought not to.'" (*1 Timothy 5:12-13*). Because women tend to spend a lot of time in each other's homes and work closely with other women, they observe situations which can become distorted in the telling and retelling. Paul states that widows get into the habit of going from home to home, looking for something to occupy their idleness. Idle hands are the devil's workshop, and God cautions against allowing idleness to enter our lives. "A gossip betrays a confidence; so avoid a man [or woman] who talks too much." (*Proverbs 20:19*).

One day I lied to my Aunt Ruby about cleaning. She started whooping me on my hand with a white-handled knife, and accidently cut me. I stopped crying, and told her she had cut me. She started screaming, "Stop lying!" She picked up a broom, and smacked it against my head and body. I don't think she knew how much she'd hurt me.

Up to then I'd loved her so much. She'd been the only one who taught me anything. I showed the marks to my mom. She said nothing, but a few months later we moved to Columbus, Ohio. My Ohio cousins hated Alabama.

CHAPTER 4

When we first moved to Ohio we lived with my Aunt Brenda in a low-income apartment. She was my favorite aunt. She was always drunk, and everybody came to her house to hang out. All the cousins there hung around people in their age group. It was only natural that I bonded with a cousin around my own age.

This was Bryan. His mother and my mom were close, so we became good friends. He knew a lot more about Ohio then I did. Anytime we got together with his family, Bryan and I would stay out all night, chasing girls, breaking into apartments and stealing booze. This took me further away from my true path.

One night, when my mother went out with a man named Jessie, I stayed with Bryan and his mom. I was excited; I knew his mom wasn't going to bother us. When I arrived at his house, I skipped up the stairs, only to be stopped by a cute brown puppy. I played with it for a while, and then started down the hallway to his room.

When I walked into his room, sticking out from underneath a mountain of clothes was what appeared to be a bed. Bryan sat on a metal milk crate beside the bed listening to the radio. He pushed the clothes with his right arm, uncovering dog poop that he had allowed to stack up on his bed and floor. Bryan got off the milk crate and said, "Sit here" I was so relieved not to have to sit on the floor. The smell was so repulsive it made my stomach turn.

We started talking about the girls he had played "hide and go get it" with. He told tell me how he took them to a graveyard and did it with them. I would occasionally shake my head in agreement, like I knew what he was talking about. I had never even kissed a girl before, so I really had no idea. He told me stories of girls he wanted to sleep with in the neighborhood. Then he would tell me about girls he thought would be great for me.

Shortly after we started talking, his mom came upstairs and said she was going to our Aunt Brenda's apartment across the street. Before she left she started screaming at him about his room. She wanted him to clean it. She then calmly asked if I was hungry. When I said I was, she ordered him to make me some pizza. Though Bryan was only two years older than me, he seemed to carry the weight of the world on his shoulders. For a moment

I wondered if my marble could bring him peace. But this was my marble.

The Doctor said, "So how does the marble make you feel?"

"It's the only thing that has been with me from the beginning." Daniel responded, slipping it into his top pocket.

We cleaned the entire house. He told me what to do, and I did most of the work. His mother was very particular about the way she wanted things done. Though she was fat, lazy and smoked a lot of weed, she was nice to me, so I didn't care how she treated him.

After we cleaned he put a pizza in the microwave and made some Kool-Aid. He did it exactly the way his mom had told him to. I helped as much as I could, taking no shortcuts. I knew she would beat him if something wasn't done right.

After the rigorous cleaning, and filling our stomachs, he suggested we take a bath. We were having a very cold winter, so turning up the heat, and getting in a hot bath was something I couldn't refuse. Bryan went upstairs and started running the water. A few minutes later he told me to go ahead and take a bath. I put my hand in the scorching hot water. "Aw shit," I said, felling this was way too hot.

When he started to get undressed, I headed for the door.

"Man, we took baths together before," he protested.

Though that was true, I still felt uncomfortable. Finally I took my clothes off. I gritted my teeth as I put my feet in the nearly scalding water. When I started to sit I jumped up, saying: "Fuck this. I'll take a bath after you."

I went to his room and started playing with his radio. With my left hand I fiddled with the marble. It was yellow. I noticed the plug had been cut and taped, so I hooked one of the wires to the metal milk crate. When he came out of the bathroom he was half naked still drying off. I said "Damn, cuz, couldn't you have done that in the bathroom?"

"Shut up," he said, laughing. He headed downstairs. "Watch this," he said as he returned. He pulled out a jar of peanut butter. He opened his towel, called the dog over, and made it look as if the dog were licking his penis. I turned my head away in disgust. He said I should put peanut butter on my privates, but by then I was walking away. I felt sorry for the dog.

When Bryan came in the room and sat his naked wet ass on the crate, I touched the radio wires to the crate. He hit the floor, and a huge spark lit the room. He'd laughed all through the time he was messing with the dog, which made this even funnier to me.

He tried to tackle me, but I took off down the stairs. I heard his breathing behind me. Suddenly his laughter stopped, replaced by frantic panting. I got to the kitchen, still gripping my marble in my hand. It had turned red: danger. I turned, and saw him still on the stairs, grabbing his chest. I leapt over the couch, and rushed to him.

"Cuz, cuz, are you alright?"

He had a hard time talking, because he couldn't breathe. I was scared to death. Calling 9-1-1 could get us both in trouble. I picked him up, threw his arm over my shoulders, and we headed for the door.

As we reached the parking lot, his body grew really heavy. I had to do something, so I pulled his hand down, bent lower, and slung his entire body over my shoulders. He began to hyperventilate, so I ran, picking my feet up high to get through the snow. My aunt's house seemed far away, but we finally got there.

I banged on the door. It opened, and as I hit the floor with him, I could smell the weed. Somebody pushed me out the way, grabbed a bag and handed it to him. He started to breath in it, and somehow caught his breath. They gave him a blanket and told him to sit up.

"How did this happen?" his mother demanded. "What did you do to get an asthma attack?"   "We were just playing," I said.

We returned to their house, where his mom had his inhaler in her purse. Once he'd started recovering, she began to yell at him.

We went upstairs to bed. Bryan said I could have made him fall and hit his head outside. I paid him no mind. I assumed he was just embarrassed. Somehow we got to talking about the cremation place right behind the projects. The smell of burning bodies really made me sick. I wanted to go home. I started crying. A half hour later my mom came back, crying, from her date. As we left, we started comforting each other.

A couple of weeks later we moved in with my Aunt Polly. Polly smoked a lot of weed, but she was funny when she was high. Though Mom and Polly partied together, they encouraged each other to take care of business. Bryan and his mom visited sometimes. Bryan would play games that always ended with him trying to get the girls out of their clothes, especially our cousin Marsha. He'd already tried to have sex with our younger cousin, Becky. I tried to keep him away from our cousin Linda. When he tried it with Marsha and me, we told him no.

Marsha was a couple years younger, but she was smart. I liked smart people, and respected her. When Marsha and I started keeping our distance from Bryan, he got scared. I knew the things he was doing were wrong. Becky, a bright young girl who was always reading, might've become another one of his victims. I remember several attempts. Did he ever succeed? I don't know.

"Are these normal events in your family?" the Doctor asked.

"I'm not sure," Daniel said uneasily, "but I always wondered if people knew or even cared. I think most of the girls would've thought it was their fault. Bryan's mom was always hard on him. When it came to him doing something that would make her look bad, she would deny it and become furious."

I often found myself sitting in the closet, puzzled. I never thought of what to do next. If we weren't playing games, we were talking about girls. One afternoon, when we were supposed to be napping, he talked on and on about girls. I told him about a smart, intelligent girl I'd met. I was always attracted to that type. Linda's mother, my Aunt Polly, came in and whipped us both for talking. I didn't even have time to run under the bed.

My mother, sister and I moved in with a man named Jessie. My second sister, Ashley, had just been born, and Mom felt it was time for a change.

Jessie was a light-skinned guy who was good at dealing drugs. He always had nice cars and connections. He played real gangster music that disrespected women. He played songs like "Too Short Bitches Ain't Shit but Hoes and Tricks" I'd never heard so much cussing in songs. I didn't think he was ready for kids.

One day we left the house, as well as our furniture. I just thought we were moving to find a better life, but I later learned Jessie had shot a man in South Park over drugs. We hid in some apartments outside of Columbus, Ohio. Bryan, his mom, and Aunt Brenda would visit from time to time. Bryan and I would break into apartments and race each other. Though I was faster, our other cousin, Linda had me beat.

When Jessie left for California, we had to wait until summer, when school let out. With Bryan gone to his grandfather's in Cleveland, I was left alone. I hung out with our neighborhood's Mexican gangs, doing all I could to impress them. One school morning I noticed a blue Toyota speeding my way. I walked into the middle of the street. Just as he was about to make a right turn, I stopped. He swerved, clipping the back of my pants. We laughed as the driver ran off the road onto the curb. He stayed in his car and we walked away. One of my new friends, Little Puppet, and his sister gave me a ride to school that day.

After school I went to Little Puppet's house and met his sisters. One was seventeen, and other nineteen. They both had very long hair. They would both tease me sexually. Not caring about how old I was, they were impressed by my thug persona. Every day I went to Little Puppet's apartment, only to be snatched up by his sisters. They cooked really good eggs and rice.

One evening I went over there to see if Little Puppet was home.

The Doctor asked, "Why do they call him Little Puppet?"

"Don't know, Doc. Didn't' ask."

I knocked on the door. His sister, Maria answered. "Come in" she said. She stood, her blonde hair, highlighted with black strands. She was a short, brown-skinned girl of about 130 pounds. She wore blue khakis, and had a blue bandana wrapped around her forehead. Her black top lifted her boobs, exposing her belly ring. I had to keep myself from staring at her.

She said motioned toward the couch, and said: "Sit." She brought me juice and the remote for the TV, but she wasn't being as funny as she'd been when her heavyset sister was around. She looked pissed off.

Having learned a few Spanish words, I said: "Que Pasa?"

She smiled and sighed, "Nada. Little Puppet should be here soon, okay?" Then she went into her room.

I waited for maybe ten minutes, and then told Maria I was going to leave. Little Puppet had warned me not to mess with his sisters, but I assumed he was kidding. After all, they were the ones doing the flirting. Now Maria called me to the back room. I found her lying on the bed with one hand behind her head, and the other moving under the blanket between her legs.

"Come here, poppy. I want to show you something," she said.

I thought she was just messing with me, like she and her sister had done when they'd kissed in front of me. The last time they'd embarrassed me, they'd joked about a black boy blushing. So this time I did what she said, and sat on the bed.

Maria asked: "Do you want to touch me?"

I nodded, and placed my hand on her stomach. She moaned. I knew it was an act, but didn't care. She licked her lips. She pulled her hand from underneath the covers, showing me a blue toy that looked like a huge blue Smurf penis. She turned the head and it started to vibrate. When she put it back under the covers, she rocked her body. She tried to knock my hand down there, but I resisted. Though my heart beat faster and faster, I tried to show no emotion.

A noise came from the front room. As I jumped up, her sister met me at the bedroom door. They began to argue and cry in Spanish. I didn't understand much. Maria's sister screamed, "Keep your hands off my stuff, Punta!" When their mom came, and jumped into the argument, I left.

The next day after school, as I was walking home from the bus stop, Little Puppet ambushed me. He hit me in the back of my head. I was shocked. I turned around, and tried to ask him what was up.

"We have to fight hommie," he told me.

We fought toe-to-toe. I punched him in the face and he hit the ground and got right back up. He didn't give up. I was tiring. I stepped back, and spit out a razor blade that I kept in the left side of my mouth for protection. I told him that we were friends and I was loyal. If he wanted blood, I'd give it to him. I proceeded to slice the crook of my arm. Blood seeped out. He backed away and called me crazy. "Our friendship is still over," he told me. I went home. I told my mom I didn't know who'd beat me up. She took me to the hospital. We left Ohio. My friends nicknamed me "Crazy Loc."

The Doctor Interjected, "Daniel, I am sorry to cut you off, but we are taking longer than I expected, and we need to stop for the day."

"So, Sir, do I come back later, or tomorrow?" Daniel asked.

"Neither," said the Doctor. "We will continue with our sessions every Friday, if that's okay with you."

"I don't really have a choice; obviously I won't be going anywhere."

"Unfortunately I will need to have the marble back," the Doctor said.

Daniel sadly returned the marble and left the office.

CHAPTER 5

It was the same routine every day, eating and studying philosophy. The people in there are really unwell. I don't know how much time was passing and struggled to remember the story. Friday came around. I was reunited with my marble.

The Doctor asked, "How's it been going Daniel?"

"Well, I hate this place that's for sure." Daniel responded.

"I understand," said the Doctor. "Let's try to get through this. Please start from where you left off."

Driving to California when I was eleven was crazy. We traveled across the country in December, in a half-working car. The car had no heat, so my mother would constantly smoke cigarettes to keep us warm, so she said. It was a long couple of days, but I did enjoy the view, driving through the mountains and open plains. When we got there we moved into an apartment in Long Beach. It was beautiful. The Mexican culture there was very different from that in Ohio. The people were interesting, and I was fascinated.

Jessie would leave for days at a time, but other than that, it felt like we were a family. We ate together, celebrated holidays and made new friends. Then one day Jessie never returned. We were forced to move in with my Grandmother in Inglewood, in Los Angeles. It was a two-bedroom apartment, with nine people in it. My Islamic grandmother was upset with my mother. She'd warned my mom about living with a non-Muslim man and not being married, and felt Mom hadn't listened.

When we'd first arrived out there, my mother had enrolled in nursing school, but in our new situation she was forced to stop, so she could take care of all of us. That included her siblings. We ate potatoes in any form you could think of, for breakfast, lunch and dinner. They blamed my Uncle Jamal and I for anything and everything. We had to sleep in the same bed. One morning I woke up to a wet spot in the bed. When I looked up, my uncle was pointing at me, and suddenly my grandma was beating me. That's when I learned that my uncle had a bladder problem.

Despite the bladder problems, my two uncles were gangsters! They introduced me to their gang. They hung around bad people like Big Slim, Milky Way and few others. They called themselves the "East Side Lendwood Pulp Street Crips." Blue was their color. It didn't make much sense, because when they got into fights, their opponents often wore blue too. The gangbangers fought over territories, who could sell drugs, and where, and to whom they could sell them. They were the first to say: It's always about money, power and respect.

They were scum. Jamal's older brother, my Uncle Johnny, told me how a 15-year-old girl wanted to be part of the gang. When she came over to smoke some weed, five guys took turns raping her. Johnny bragged how he was the first one to have sex with her, and how he made her bleed. His friends rapped about how he "popped her cherry." They would stay out all night hustling and killing, often all night and into the next day.

Johnny would come in early in the morning and grab a bag of crack from his stash. One day I was curious and went into his stash. I saw a bag of rocks and a pistol. That's when I knew for sure my uncles were gangsters. Although I knew what took place at night, they never let me get too involved in the street life. Once Johnny came in covered in blood.

The big hommies from the hood, or my uncle's gang, had Jamal and me get into stuff like breaking into schools and stealing computers. Soon our missions escalated, and they had us beating up people that came through our neighborhood. We robbed people, and stole cars. My favorite aunts were my mom's sisters, Nancy and Shawna. No matter what I did, they always had my back.

I learned that life would be easier if I just practiced the Islamic faith. Once a year we would go thirty days only eating or drinking after the sun went down. When my mother saw me becoming a Muslim, she got us a place of our own a couple apartments down.

I felt confused. As my beliefs changed, my grandma and mom had different rules. At grandma's I never ate pork. Yet at home my mom expected me to eat anything she served me, including pork. Then on Christmas my mom bought everyone presents, including her siblings at Grandma's. When they took their gifts next door, my grandmother got upset. She stopped speaking to my mom. Eventually we moved back to Ohio, and in with our Aunty Polly in Columbus.

CHAPTER 6

Things had changed in Ohio. Bryan had moved to Cleveland, so it was just Polly's kids and me. We played all the time. One day we played so hard that I fell off the swing, hit my head, and lay in a coma for two days. I dreamed I was being sucked into a vacuum, and then I floated through a vortex of colors. The colors reminded me of the primary colors I had seen in the woods. At first I was relaxed, happy to be going somewhere that felt safe. Then a voice said, "It is not time yet." I got scared, and struggled to return. I don't remember much else, but when I woke up my mother had taken my necklace from around my neck. I never got it back, I was so glad it wasn't my marble. I also recall waking up in the basement, and seeing a mirror, a razor blade, white residue, and a straw under the edge of the waterbed. I didn't know what they were for.

My cousin Linda and I always played in the basement. We were beginning to get very close, when one day, when I was lying in the water bed, she came downstairs. She said she wanted to show me something. She wanted to play house.

"I'm the mommy and you're the daddy," she said.

I was stuck at first, She was a very pretty girl, but not in a sexual way. She was intelligent and artistic. Now she stood over me and took off her clothes. When I looked at my marble it was turning yellow. I was confused. She bent over me, squatting, and headed downward. As she got lower I could smell her. She was a sweaty, nervous girl, and to be honest, it smelled like piss.

Just as she spread her lips apart, I mumbled, "What are you doing?" I sounded like I felt: disappointed. Just like that she stopped. I felt relieved. She took off upstairs in a slow sprint. We never really spoke again after that, but I've always wondered what she was thinking. Who had taught her that? She knew more then I did about sex but I was older. We were never close again. Was this the reason?

"I don't know, because this is only the second time I've ever talked about it,"
said Daniel.

The Doctor asked Daniel, "When was the first time you talked about it?"

"The first was years later, with Bryan. He was disappointed that I hadn't gone
through with it. He pretty much stated that he would've done it. I could not understand
what was going on in his mind. I told Bryan that Linda and I always played marbles on
the front porch, and one time I cracked the window with my marble and she took the
blame." As Daniel told the Doctor this, he looked at the chip on his marble. "The chip
on my marble will forever remind me," he said.

When Bryan returned home from Cleveland, he moved back in
with his mom. I would occasionally stay with them. The first week he was
home I caught him having sex with a girl I'd told him I had a crush on. I
still remained a virgin. I became their lookout. When I looked at my marble
it turned green: jealousy and envy. He banged the girl I'd thought of as my
future wife in the grass.

Bryan had a thing for the girls, and he knew how to persuade
people, but he never used this talent for anything positive. On one of my
overnight visits, he introduced me to a 19 year old girl named Angie. She
drove a small blue convertible. At this point Bryan was only about fourteen.

When Angie first pulled into the driveway of his mom's house, he grabbed the keys.

Angie was attractive. She was a white girl, but I could see from the way she acted that she had some black in her. Bryan said she was his Uncle Sydney's girlfriend. Sydney was locked up at the time. Our cousins—in particularly Rhome—had sex with her on a regular basis. When I asked if Sydney knew, Bryan said: "Yes, he wants it that way, so she won't go and leave him for somebody else. It would mess up Sydney's money if Rhome didn't sleep with her. She's got needs too." Angie was a thief, and she would take Bryan and me on shoplifting sprees.

Bryan even got me to try to make a move on her, but I didn't know what I was doing. She turned me down fast. For some reason she gave him much more attention. I thought I would be a virgin for the rest of my life.

One day Bryan started to explain to me that almost all the cousins in the family were bisexual or gay. He added that people only care about themselves, so we had to look out for each other.

Lev 18:22-24 You shall not lie with a male as with a woman. It

is an abomination. Nor shall you mate with any animal, to

defile yourself with it. Nor shall any woman stand before an animal to mate with it. It is perversion. Do not defile

yourselves with any of these things; for by all these the

nations are defiled, which I am casting out before you.

He then offered me a drink of Boone's Farm. This was an alcoholic

beverage. There were bottles of it under his mom's fish tank. She had 12-

inch sharks in that tank. I assumed she put the tank there to protect her

stash. I was always greedy, so I drank and drank. After we'd drank half of

two bottles, and replaced the missing beverage with water, Bryan brought

out something else. It was in a small plastic bag. I thought it was baking

soda, or something. He emptied the contents onto a glass coffee table, and

spooned some baby laxative back into the bag. Bryan shook the bag tied the

end and took it to his mother's room. Bryan then took a plastic card and

smashed the white substance on the table. I asked him what it was.

"Cocaine," Bryan said with a smile. He asked me for a dollar.

Unsure of myself, I reached in my pocket, brought out the only one I had,

and gave it to him. Bryan rolled up the dollar, and used it like a straw,

snorting the cocaine up each nostril. He handed me the dollar and said:

"Your turn."

"No," I said. "There's a thing at school—DARE—and they say

this stuff is addictive."

Bryan started talking very fast. He said: "It doesn't have to be. This is how people make money. Do you like money?"

"Yes," I admitted.

"Okay. Then there's the fact that this stuff helps you think and get a lot of things done. Isn't that a good thing?"

"I guess so," I admitted.

"And do you want to lose weight and get all the girls?"

"Yes."

He went on telling me things like that. He told me all the names of people who did it. One was a girl I liked. Finally I took the dollar and tried to snort the cocaine but nothing would go up my nose. He told me to hold the other nostril and try it again. Once I'd snorted it, I got a strange feeling in my stomach and ran to the bathroom to puke.

"No, don't," Bryan said, following me in there. "Hold it in." But I couldn't stop. I threw up all over my shirt.

"I still feel really sick," I said.

"That's okay," said Bryan. "Just do a little more. It'll make you feel better."

I followed his instructions, and I did feel better. First my stomach settled, and I didn't feel anything at all. We got more out of the bag and did it again.

Daniel looked at the Doctor then squeezed his marble.

The Doctor said, "Just remember Daniel alcohol is a gateway drug. If you can't control your drinking you can easily find yourself doing a stronger drug. You shouldn't have been drinking at that age anyway."

"I know but that's not all that happened to me" Daniel responded.

The Doctor sat up, leaning toward Daniel. "What happened?"

Bryan got our talk back on the subject of my cousins, and how they'd been willing to do almost any sexual stuff just to get what they wanted. He said it was disgusting. "We have to know if we are gay, right? And we're cousins so if we try it a little on each other, we would know for ourselves." I told him no. I tried to laugh it off, but I could see in his eyes that he wasn't joking. As I listened to all the things he said, I started questioning my own sexuality. I didn't think there was any way I could be gay.   "I think about girls all day," I told him.

"Well, we need to find out," he said, as if that settled it.

He then took me upstairs to the attic. There he had a tent all set up. We got under it, and he began to sodomize me. It was so painful that I begged him to stop. I don't know how he held me down. I guess when you're in that much pain you don't think straight… or maybe it was the drugs. I didn't know if I was bleeding or what. All I knew was that it was torture. I guess it was a lot like having hot cooking grease spilled in me. I felt that my manhood must surely be gone. As he pinned my shoulder to the floor, I felt sorry for anybody who wanted this shit. Then I heard him say: "I'm not going all the way in."

I begged him to stop, and started to cry. That's when his mama's boyfriend came into the house. I heard him come up the stairs, and I knew he must see what Bryan was doing to me. When I looked up, he was glaring at Bryan.

"Take out the trash, like your mom said." Those were his only words. He turned, and went back down the stairs. I felt totally sober, alone and confused.

"Have you ever told anyone this before?" the Doctor asked in a soothing tone. He looked as if he felt Daniel's pain.

"No," said Daniel, and he pressed his marble to his face. Daniel felt depressed, angry, and stressed, all at the same time. Looking at the marble, it was black. "I just want to continue sir, if you don't mind."

I worked with his mom's boyfriend, selling copper tubing under the table. *Why didn't he help me?* I wondered. *How could he just walk away?* I threw up again. My stomach hurt and I wanted to die! I repeat I wanted to die. His mom's boyfriend left again to drop off some copper.

I felt nothing but rage toward Bryan. I said I was going to tell. He'd hurt me and that wasn't right.

"Nobody's going to believe you," he said. He was so sure of himself, that soon I was convinced he was right. He gave me some pills for the pain. They worked right away. He said they were his mom's pills. I wanted him to feel the same kind of pain, but I couldn't do what he'd done. My body just didn't want it. As I tried to think of something that would hurt him, I broke down and cried again. He said I was acting like a girl.

I ran to his mom's room and locked myself in. He chased me, and called through the door that I would get in trouble if I got caught in there. I opened the drawer on the nightstand, and grabbed the bag of cocaine. In the movies I'd seen people flush this stuff. I could do that. Bryan continued to talk through the locked door. I notice a pistol in the nightstand, a .44 Cal. I pulled it out. I sat down on the bed, and fumbled with the pistol until the side came open. There were six bullets in it.

I thought to myself: *We should both die because we're going to hell anyway.*

I heard Bryan call out that he was going to leave. He said he was telling his mom I was in her room. I took all the bullets out but one. I swung the bedroom door open, and in one quick move I put the gun to his head. Finally I saw the fear in his eyes. He needed to understand that fear.

He cried: "Man what are you doing?"

"I'm going to fucking kill you," I told him.

"If you shoot me everybody's going to hate you forever."

I pushed and shoved him along. We went out of the house, into the backyard, where there was a shallow lake.

I got right to the edge of the water, and put the gun barrel to my head. "I'm pulling this trigger. If this gun goes off on me, you can tell your mom and my mom that I did it because I didn't want to live anymore."

Bryan stared, his jaw dropping. He thought the .44 Cal was fully loaded. Actually I only had the one bullet in it. I spun the cylinder, which turned smoothly. The steel barrel was cold against my head. Bryan started to cry.

"Do you care about me?" I asked him.

He couldn't answer.

"Why did you do that to me?" I asked.

He stared at me. "You came upstairs too."

"But I asked you to stop, and you didn't," I said. "The only thing you care about now is that you might get in trouble."

The fear in his eyes was fading. "Go ahead," he said. "Do it."

I pulled the hammer back.

"It's empty anyways," he muttered.

I heard the click, and the slam of the hammer. I hadn't even realized I was doing it.

Bryan started crying again. I stuck the gun barrel in his face. "Go into the water, Bryan," I said. "No," he sobbed. "You're going to have to kill me here. This is so fucked up. Please... I won't tell anybody."

"I know," I said. I pulled the hammer back. I could feel the round setting itself into place, ready for shooting. "Do you pray, Bryan?"

"Please, Daniel, don't."

"Oh, you're begging me now?" I thought shooting him would satisfy me, but now I realized it would only make me more upset. "I don't want to be like you anymore," I said. "You're a really bad person, Bryan."

"Please let me live," he whispered. "I'll change."

"You better," I said. I pointed the gun at a spot near his leg. It went off. I didn't shoot him that day.

The next day I woke up on the couch. Bryan was in the kitchen cooking pancakes. His mom walked downstairs and started yelling at him about cooking all the food. She started crying and screaming at him. She turned to me and said, "Daniel, you can't stay the night tonight."

"I'm okay with that," I replied. I thought to myself: *Fucking crazy ass people.*

From then on there was a distance between Bryan and me. He hung out with the other cousins, like Rhome and Luke. Eventually Rhome went to prison for several felonies, including sexually assaulting a girl. I didn't care after that. I never told anybody because I was afraid that people might call me gay, or say that I was a liar. When my mom decided to move back to Alabama, I was glad to leave.

CHAPTER 7

The people in our family in the south were happy to have us back in Alabama. For the first couple of weeks I didn't even have to do any strenuous chores. Then it started again: cutting down trees, picking up dog crap, and anything else they could think up to keep me busy. I got used to it.   My cousin Luke and his friends came down south for a family reunion. Luke was a light-skinned bisexual cross-dresser, about 5'6", and 165 pounds. Some younger cousins and I were outside playing in front of the Big House when a silver Mitsubishi pulled up. Two men and a woman stepped out. They talked loud, and acted excited. I figured they must have lots of energy stored up from the drive. I kept playing with my cousins. I wasn't worried. With everybody there, I thought we were going to have a great time.

When I ran into the house to get water, I heard people in the bathroom talking and laughing. One of Luke's friends, a tall dark, black man of about 200 pounds, came out twisting his hips. He was trying to buckle up his pants, but they were too tight. I thought it was funny. Standing in the kitchen, I drank my water and gawked at him.

Our aunts and uncles congregated in the living room. Aunt Polly, from Ohio knocked on the bathroom door. "Luke, boy, what are yall doing?" she called.

"Nothing… puttin' on my swim suit," he replied in a soft voice. He sounded like he was chuckling. Sexual noises and laughter came from the other side of the door.

The adults started getting angry. Aunt Ruby's' daughter, my cousin Brandy, who was about ten years older than me, shooed me outside with the back of her hand. I went back out, wondering why so many men were in the bathroom. And where was that woman who'd been with them?

A few minutes later I wanted to show my cousins how I could flip off the second floor patio. I went in the house. As I walked upstairs I noticed the woman sitting on the edge of the bed in Little Dustin's room. It was my cousin Luke crying and ranting.

"Fuck them," he sniffed. "I don't need this shit." I hesitated not knowing how to approach the situation. I could feel his pain. I figured he must feel as if he just didn't belong.

The Doctor asked, "How was your relationship with him?"

"I didn't know him that well," said Daniel, "but I knew he was being treated different for whatever it was that he believed in, a lot like what had happened to me."

"And what did you believe in?" the Doctor inquired.

Daniel responded, "I believe that all people should be treated equal, and I believe that people should be able to express themselves the way they want to as long as it did not cause others harm."

When we'd been in Ohio, Luke always had a lot of money. He was the one who organized the family gatherings. Once he held one at a nice hotel. There was this incident where I almost drowned in the pool. Bryan sat there, just watching, as I struggled and reached for help. I thought I was dead. I gave up. When my body floated to the top, Luke pulled me out. I was crying. He'd saved me from what seemed like certain death. Now he needed me. As he stood there with his wig in his hand, I walked up to him, and told him it would be okay.

"Daniel," he said sadly, "you don't understand."

"I know," I said. "People fear what they don't understand. But even though I don't understand this, you are still my cousin."

He smiled. "Thanks."

It was all I could say to him. I walked away, concealing my own thoughts. I knew I would probably get in trouble just for talking to him.

He left that day for California. After he left, the adults got mean. They gave all us kids chores to do, then sat back and talked about him. Over the next couple of days my other cousins kept their distance from the house. My mother would've beat me if I'd run away, so I was left with their work. My cousins would soon return to their own towns.

Down there I got tired of all the strict treatment. I started to rebel. Once again, all I wanted to do was find out about sex. We had a sex education class in school, but it taught me nothing. I was too embarrassed to ask my friends. I wanted to know how it felt inside a woman. I messed up in school, and my grades suffered because I wasn't focused. I knew what would happen if I came home with bad grades. My teachers had already called several times about my grades and behavior. My mother had already warned me.

No one would help me with my studies. When I asked for help with my homework, my aunts and uncles said I was stupid, and wouldn't amount to anything. But I knew the truth: they couldn't help me. They couldn't even do simple division. On the day I came home with a failing report card, my mother sat on the couch and gave me an evil look. She started to cry. She said it was so hard to raise a child by herself. *Then why did she keep having kids?*

She tied me to a pole on the kitchen nook leading to the ceiling. I cried and begged, "No, mom please don't! I love you!" As she tied my hands with an extension cord, I tried to imagine myself in another place, but I was far too scared. As I reached for my marble she grabbed me. She'd beaten me with extension cords on many occasions, but now she was tying me up with them. I hadn't noticed the switches she had ready on the couch.

She cried as she asked: "Why won't you get good grades? Why do you get in so much trouble?" She hit my face, then beat me all over my body. I started to bleed. I wanted to tell her, but I knew she wouldn't stop. I tried to loosen the restraints enough to reach for my marble. She hit me harder. I jumped over the breakfast nook, but she met me on the other side and punched me. Her switches got caught under my arm and broke.

"Okay, motherfucker!" she raged. Picking up a broom, she beat me as she would a murderer, thief, or rapist. She thrashed me until I stopped moving. I fell on the floor with my hands above me, still tied to the breakfast nook pole. Finally she finished. She walked to the backroom and closed the door. Using my teeth, I undid one of the knots, releasing myself from the pole.

I ran out the door and through the woods. I got another beating from tree limbs and thorn bushes. I felt as if someone was chasing me, wanting to kill me. When I came out of the woods, I was relieved to see a police station. I went through the front entrance, crying and cut up. I didn't need their sympathy. I just wanted them to listen. But the police didn't care about my injuries. Within an hour they'd released me back to my "guardians."

"What kind of bruises did you have?" The Doctor asked, sitting up in his chair.

"I was covered from head-to-toe with swollen welts. My eyes had been blackened and my nose swollen. There was blood on my shirt. I'd been torn apart, inside and out."

The Doctor shook his head sadly. "I'm sorry, Daniel."

When I returned home, my Uncle Bill tied me to a weight bench. Bill made my older cousin Terrance watch as he pushed the switches into my rectum. He said this was to show me how they would treat me in prison. "Get used to it," he said.

I could tell my cousin Terrance, didn't approve. He hung his head in sorrow. I felt badly for him because he had to watch this. Afterwards I was so filled with anger that I almost made a move on my cousin Pam.

"Let's play house" I suggested.

She agreed, but I quickly came back to reality. This was not the right way to get revenge.

After that I felt as if nobody could hurt me anymore. I thought about burning the house down. When my mom came upstairs, she gave me a look as if to say, "I'm sorry." But she never said anything. She just looked at me and walked away. A month later we moved into a single-wide trailer in the backyard of the Big House. It was her way of regaining our independence, but she didn't tell me that.

It had two bedrooms. We shared water and power with the Big House, connecting our sewer pipes to theirs and tapping into the water lines. For a couple of weeks we used long yellow extension cords from the Big House for power.

One day as I sat in the living room playing marbles, the chipped marble turned orange. I felt filled with enthusiasm. The windows started to rattle, like the trailer was falling apart. I thought it was going to fall off its slanted foundation and roll over. As I opened the door, I saw a blue

Cadillac. It was Jessie, my mom's boyfriend from Ohio. The moment I saw him I figured all my suffering would stop. My mom would not try to impress anyone anymore—not with him there. From the car he pulled a huge brown puppy. It had the biggest head I ever saw on a dog. He said it was a bull mastiff.

Jessie stayed for a couple of days. While he was there my sisters and I were allowed to do whatever we wanted. All we wanted was to play with my new dog, I walked her everywhere. He told my mom he was going to leave for the weekend. After he'd gone my mother asked me whether she should marry him. I said yes, but he never returned.

Jessie left the dog. I named her Destiny, after a girl I had a crush on. My Uncle Bill took her from me and changed her name to Daphne, so I hung her. I didn't want him to have anything that belonged to me, and I didn't want her to have to suffer as I did. She survived, and my mother gave me a cat instead. We called him Snowball. He didn't make it. When he scratched my sister, I put him in a trash bag and tossed him in the middle of the road to be run over. I threw the bag in the woods. I informed my sister, and I think she told our mom. Then I had to see a mental doctor. The Doctor asked me questions, and had me look at pictures so I could identify them. I saw the Doctor a few times, but never told him anything. I could see my mom looking at us from behind glass. I didn't trust the Doctor. I thought if I had told him anything I would get another beating.

He asked my mom if she, or any other family member, had ever been told they had mental illnesses. He thought my depression and aggression might be genetic. She said no. Soon we stopped going to him. It was assumed that I would outgrow my marble. I rarely looked at it. I put it in a hole in the wood, underneath the carpet in the corner of the closet. It was the only thing that I could keep safe.

D.K. Charley

THIS PAGE LEFT INTENTIONALLY BLANK

CHAPTER 8

I turned to the street gangs thinking that they were going to protect me and love me. I associated myself with a local gang. They were mostly young boys known as The organization. They wore black and their symbols were a pitchfork and six point stars, distinguishing them from other groups. The Organization preferred the word "organization" over "gang." Most of them became like brothers to me. We called each other "boss" or "kinfolk."

When I stopped listening to my mom, she decided it would be best if I spent weekends in a juvenile facility. The strangest thing about the place was that it was mostly people who had committed crimes, not people who disobeyed their parents. At that point I felt like I had no hope. Every weekend I got closer with the people there. Every Friday I would return to the same inmates. Some waited months to be sentenced. Other just came for weekends, or every other weekend, but they were there for breaking the law; it was like a school of crime. There I learned more about gangs than I had on the street.

A guy named Larry Hoover had started it out of Chicago, but I didn't know why. The organization members wore their right pant leg up in jail until the staff caught on. One of my cell mates told me he was a King Gangster Disciple. He taught me a lot of about the organization. It was difficult for me. Growing up I'd wanted to be a part of my uncle's gang, the Crips, mainly because blue was my favorite color. Compared to the Nation, Organization had more knowledge, while the Crips just understood about street life.

The initiation consisted of me falling on my back several times, with my hands across my chest, so I wouldn't break my fall. I did this six times until blood seeped from my head. My cellmates had a test for me to learn. At the end of a long brutal enlightening, I noticed a group of inmates had rushed into the cell. They debated whether to beat me or not. My cellmate said no. The Organization were still cool with the Crips. I liked that.

They called the two affiliations: "eight ball." The sign was a pitchfork and a "c" facing each other. I learned how to stack gang signs and how to make people follow my orders. If I had mentioned how much I loved my uncle and his gang, I would've been called a flip-flop, so I said nothing about Crips. I remember one weekend a guy was masturbating and I got annoyed. I tried to put the pillow over my head to block him out, but he got louder. It was like he was taunting me. I was frustrated. I'd never had sex, and didn't have the urge to masturbate. I felt he was being disrespectful. I told him to wait to masturbate when I went out for snack. He told me to leave him alone. He held his low-rider magazine and continued. That night I had five guys run into my cell and beat him. They cracked his head on the metal toilet bolted to the wall. It was quick. They took him out of my cell, and placed into a cell of his own. Sunday came and I was home again.

The Doctor asked: "Why do you think people join gangs?"

"I don't know, Doc," Daniel replied. "Everyone's situation is different. I think when you're younger you're looking for someone to look up to, and you're looking for a family. Maybe you're searching for a hidden path. Maybe your father or role model was a well-known gang member. You want all the luxuries he has, and figure you'll get them the same way he did, instead of following your own path. Or maybe you needed protection. I think that when you become a man you don't have to fight for what other people believe in, but what you believe in. Your loyalty should always be to yourself first. Very few situations are clear. Somebody's entire family is of a certain gang. Something bad happens, and they seek revenge, not knowing that every act of violence perpetuates the cycle. In my case, I had all the ingredients for membership. You know, Doc, maybe some people just like the color.

One morning while waiting for the school bus, my cousin Terrance and I got drunk and smoked some weed. I was really high because I didn't do drugs that often. It was Terrance's first time. As we sat at the back of the bus, a high school student called me a doughnut. He was disrespecting my organization. I was in middle school and he was a big guy, so I wasted no time in jumping on top of him. I swung hard, left then right, back and forth, rhythmically. I wasn't going to stop but someone pulled me off. I stood in the aisle waiting for him to do something. The bus stopped suddenly. I flew backwards. He jumped on top of me and started pounding on my face. I didn't feel a thing. The bus driver broke it up and told me to sit in the front.

When we pulled up to my middle school, the principal was waiting. We got off the bus, ready to fight again, but I could tell he was embarrassed. He was five years older than me.

"Come on," he told me.

"Calm down," I said. "I'm finished for now."

He cried. I laughed, thinking that, because he was older, he was going to get in trouble. Instead I got suspended, but he didn't. My mom beat me with a paddle.

That evening the bus pulled up in front of the Big House and Terrance stepped out. Four other guys stepped out behind him. Terrance took off his shirt and began to fight. I jumped off the patio with my grandfather's .32 caliber revolver. I'd been keeping it with me upstairs. When I got out to the street, I saw it was people I'd hung out with before I got locked up. I pulled the gun from under my shirt, held up the distress sign, and said: "What's up, Fam?"

"Naw, fam, it aint goin be none of that," they said. "You fucked with our fam."

I put down the gun and jumped in. I hit one in the face. Another attacked me and we fell on the ground. I rolled on top and started punching him. The first guy got back on me and started kicking. I had his friend and wouldn't let go. Our neighbor came out and said that she was going to call the police. We stopped. Just like that, it was over, and they walked away. They were madder at Terrance then they were at me.

My aunt and uncle brought me inside and started cussing at me. I told them that I was fighting my own gang and they told me I was too stupid to be in a gang. I would soon prove them wrong.

When I got suspended from school I returned to the juvenile facility. There I reunited with friends who were carjackers. The white boys liked to set fire to things when they got mad. I didn't associate too much with the arsonists. Most of my friends were murderers, robbers, drug dealers, and kidnappers. Most of them did what I said because of my other friends, and who they were. That got me respect. People always offered me their food, or let me take what I wanted. But I never tried to starve anyone. I didn't have to prove I was a bad ass.

After the King of The orginazation left and was sentenced, I started disassociating myself from the Nation. I felt that they had betrayed me, when they jumped my cousin and me. I learned that there was just so much you could get away with as a child. For most crimes they only kept you in until you were 18. But the facility was becoming my second home. Sometimes I didn't want to leave. This went on for about six months. The food got better. The guards knew me by name.

When I returned to school I was placed in a special-ed class. It was because of my grades and behavior. One day a student pissed me off and I stabbed him in the hand with a number two pencil. He'd insisted on calling me "slow." The teacher said she was going to call my mom. I knew I was going to be in trouble. Though she knew the student had been picking on me, she'd refused to do anything. That's why I threatened to kill her, which made matters worse. I was sentenced to three months in juvenile detention.

It was the same place, but it was different. I knew the staff, but not the inmates, so I stayed to myself. I only spoke when I had to. My mom didn't want me to come home, so when I was released on probation I was placed in a group home. I was still only 12, but after the events of the previous year, I felt my life was over.

I went to live in a small group house in Mobile, Alabama. There were two sides, one for girls and the other for boys. Most of them went home weekends, but not me. I shared a room with two other boys. Both were Bloods. The doors had alarms hooked to them. These chirped if you opened the door. I learned how to disarm them by connecting the door to the frame with a wire. The windows had the same alarms. Even if you by got by the alarms, you could not escape the cameras in the hall. My roommates were white guys. From day one I told them I was With the organization, so they hated me. Though we agreed not to fight they did horrible things to me. One day they put a dead bird under my bed. The smell stayed in the room for four days. The two guys were 17. They went home every weekend. Having nowhere to go, I had to do their choirs on the weekends. On weekdays we were all responsible for arriving at the bus stop together. If we fought, they put us in the detention center for the weekend.

People from the group home—boys and girls who didn't care—ran the schools. In school I hooked up with people from my gang. They walked me from the group home to school. On the way back to the group home my fellow gang members beat one of my roommates up, and then ran off. That night they tried to jump me, but I was the one who went back to the detention center. When I returned I was put in my own room, and grounded for two weeks.

After two weeks one of my old roommates left, but his friend was still there. During dinner I punched him in the mouth. He hit the floor. I went to the detention center for a week but I was happy. When I came back I got more respect. The girls started to love me. They begged to see my penis. I obliged but never was able to do anything. More Organization members started to arrive. They put one in my room. I learned even more about crime and gangs. One thing I found out was that gangs in the south had more religious beliefs than gangs in California. We enlightened each other on the teachings of King David. My set recruited soldiers in a matter of weeks. We would send them on missions for drugs, or to discipline someone (beating up someone for violating rules or disrespecting us).

The gangbanger life led me to almost kill a guy for wanting out of the organization. He wanted me to do it, not the soldiers, so I took him around the side and beat him. I told him to fight back but he wouldn't. This infuriated me. I was sad afterwards, but I'd felt it had to be done. While waiting for the police to come I tried to kill myself. I ripped a sheet, tying it around the bar in a closet, and then I stood on my tiptoes. When I tried to fall it began to choke me. The bar in the closet broke. Right after that I regained consciousness. When the staff and the police came in, they called the paramedics. I was sent to the detention center where I tried again, using a plastic fork on my wrist. The pain was unbearable. I gave up. All I got was deep scratches on my wrist. I felt I was a failure.

They gave me nine months in juvenile boot camp for assault. It was set up like a military boot camp, with two sets of fences around it, both around 15 to 20 feet high. The inside fence had razor barbed wire at the top. The fence on the outside was an electrical fence.

We had to exercise every day. The only times that we didn't exercise were chow time, mail call, school, or on Sundays. We marched and ran everywhere in formation, as if we were actually in the military. Sometimes we even had drill competitions between platoons. People would sell pictures of their sisters for snacks. The ones who got the pictures would go to the bathroom and masturbate.

A lot of the female sergeants had sex with the inmates. We were all between 11 and 18. It was the most fun I'd had in a long time. Later I led a platoon.

I met another guy who was King of the organization. His looks reminded me of the devil. Something about his eyes was pure evil. I was the only person he would talk to. He was a big guy, 17, 5'7" and 200 pounds. This light-skinned boy had a pitchfork burned in his right side extremely deep. The bottom half of his body reminded me of a goat. The top part of his body was not aligned with the rest. He was diagnosed with extreme scoliosis. That explained his body's disfigurement, but not his huge misshapen head. Two knots protruded from his forehead. I knew I should not have associated with him, but being around him brought me great respect. I became so filled with power that I almost killed a guy again. The guy didn't do what I said. He kept getting us in trouble. Many times we would have to run mile after mile because of him. I hoped he would escape, but the razor wire gate deterred him. I had to do something.

The military staff put me in charge of the platoon. The King backed me up. I tried to talk to the guy who was always getting us in trouble; but he would not listen. The order was given. A bunch of people beat him. They hit him with a steel-toed boot, then smashed his head on the corner of a military bed. They dragged his lifeless body to the staff gate leaving behind a trail of blood. When I saw the wound, I felt remorse but could not show it. We all ran back, and jumped in our bunks. Somebody said he wasn't breathing, and banged on the gate. He was never seen again. The King must've been impressed. After that he taught me so much more. He assured me he would die in jail. He would stay in the boot camp until he turned 18, and then he would go to prison. He couldn't wait to go to prison where he wanted to fight King Solomon's soldiers he said. He said that the six-point star truly represented mountains. He said the war would be fought on those mountains.

The King of The organization read "Revelations" to me, and then asked to place two signs across my chest. "Prayers" he told me. "I have taught you a lot of knowledge. Now it's time for you to be enlightened by Queen Sheba." He prayed, but not to God. I closed my eyes and I saw myself walking down a yellow brick road. I even knew approximately how many bricks were on the road, though I don't know now. There was a strange, mystical woman who I feared but not in a terrifying way. She asked me questions. I did well at first, but then started to stumble. I told her: "Forgive me, Queen Sheba, I am not ready." Then I awoke. It was like being thrown from the sky. I hit the floor and ran.

Black blood poured from my eyes. I wanted to think it was a mixture of the wax and my tears on the floor. I was restrained. Guards bent my arms behind my back, and had me touch my ears with my fingers. I screamed for help. Instead they put me on medication. I had been to another world. I fell into another coma. I woke up three days later, dazed and confused. Everybody was beside me when I woke up.

"Who am I?" I asked, because I didn't know anymore.

EXODUS 20:3 "You shall have no other gods before me."

When I was released my mom and an aunt picked me up in Georgia. I stayed at a rapper's house for a couple of days. The rapper was my cousin, but he wasn't there. My mom told me to bathe with bleach, then get in the shower. This was to get the smell of jail off of me. Then we started our drive to California. There I would be put on probation. It seemed as if she was trying to find a place to

CHAPTER 9

When we got to California my grandmother had moved to Inglewood. It was a place full of "Family Swan bloods," and the gang known as Piru. My grandmother stayed in a three-bedroom house with eight people living in it, not including us. Me, my mom, and sisters made twelve. I didn't care that it was crowded. We were all family and we shared everything. In our room my uncles and I talked about everything. Johnny would be out in the streets with his gang. He couldn't wear just any color out there. On the street, black and red were for Bloods. Where I came from the Organization wore black, so this confused me. In Inglewood blue clothes were forbidden.

My mom went out looking for a job from sunup to sundown, at least, that's where she said she was. I doubted it, because she knew so many people in California.

One day I was standing outside when four guys walked right down our driveway toward me. d "What's up, Blood?" one asked.

I said nothing.

Another one said: "What set you claim? Where you from?"

My smart-ass response was, "Mobile, Alabama." I knew they were asking what gang I was in, but I'd never been in a gang. I'd been in an organization. I didn't feel like getting in trouble. I'd only been in town for a few days.

These guys walked around me like circling sharks. I moved away from the car to keep from being trapped.

"This is our hood, motherfucker," said one, and the others echoed it, throwing up gang signs.

If I said too much they would sense my hesitation. Finally I felt sure that they'd been sent there to kill me, so they'd get some rank. Did they have guns? I didn't know, but I was sure it was about to go down. I kept my eyes on the one holding his pants. I let one get in my face. Just as he did I threw him over the hood of a car. I grabbed his throat.

The other three looked stunned. They were trying to decide whether to rush me when my uncle leapt from the door, waving a broom, as he screamed: "That's my fucking nephew! I'll kill all you motherfuckers."

One guy recognized my uncle, and just like that it was over. I had no hard feelings. I gave each of them a "dap"—something like an uncivilized handshake, where your fist softly pounds the other guy's fist. Wondering what my uncle's connection was with the Bloods, I walked into the house like nothing had happened.

After my mom found a job in Long Beach, Jamal met a girl off the chat line. She was going to come by the house while everyone was at work. While we were cleaning up the room for her arrival, my older Uncle Johnny came in.

When Jamal told Johnny he was having a girl over, Johnny said: "You need to pimp her. That's what we do. After all, we're a family of pimps."

"Okay," Jamal; agreed. "I'll fuck her, pass her to you, and then we'll make her do tricks."

I heard this but I couldn't believe what I was hearing. I was in awe. I'd seen Bryan make a woman do what he wanted, but he'd never gotten them to sell themselves.

The girl was about 16, and very pretty. She had long redbone hair, fake, but it looked like hers. She had tattoos under a tight shirt, and short shorts that accentuated her figure. She also had a seductive smile.

Right after she got there, I went for a long walk. I was gone for an hour or so. When I came back to the apartment, I could smell a sticky musty odor of testosterone and estrogen: sex. Even outside the room those scents were strong. I would've peeked, but before I could, Uncle Jamal called to me to come in. She lay on the bed, looking at me. My uncle told me to turn my head while he put on his boxers.

She could see that I was nervous, and didn't know what to do. I sat down on the bed. My uncle said he was going to get a beer.

"I'll go with you," said the girl, reaching for some clothing.

"Naw," said my uncle. "You stay that way till I get back."

He went around the corner, and hid her clothes.

Once he was gone I began to worry, thinking: *What am I going to do if one of my aunts comes home?* The girl lay beneath the sheet. I could see her ass print. When I put my hand on her ass she did nothing, but I knew she was uncomfortable, so I stopped. I told her I wanted to have sex with her. She said no, my uncle would get mad. She asked if I had anything to eat. She was hungry.

I went into the kitchen and made her some noodles. As soon as I brought them in, my Uncle Jamal came in and snatched them from her. "Bitch, you don't eat unless I say so," he growled.

My mouth dropped open and I walked out the room.

Outside the room my uncle said: "Why you feed that bitch?"

"Because she was hungry," I said.

"She don't eat till she makes me money," he said, and then he ate the noodles.

I'm in way over my head, I thought to myself.

He walked into the room, faced away from me, pulled out his dick, and put it by her mouth. With no hesitation she started sucking it. "I told you this is my new hoe," he said.

The girl stayed that night in the walk-in-closet, with Jamal. When Uncle Johnny came home at six the next morning, he was upset to see her there.

"I can't believe you got her sleeping here, but not making money," he said. "You two go outside while I talk to her."

As Jamal and I drank a forty, I could see Jamal was getting upset. That's when Johnny came out to ask where the condoms were. The two of them started arguing. Johnny slapped Jamal.

"You're taking too long to swing back," he said. He looked at me, and said: "I'm just trying to help my brother, and keep him from falling in love with that girl."

I knew it was too late. After Johnny finished with her, we went back in the room. The girl was putting on her clothes back on. She'd been wearing white the day before, but now her clothes were covered in yellow cum stains. Jamal looked at her.

"I'll be back later today," she said.

"Where are you going?" he asked.

"I'm gonna get some money," she replied.

Johnny's friends were waiting outside. Without a word, he left. It was the last time I ever saw him. The girl returned that afternoon with two hundred dollars and tickets to an amusement park. Jamal gave me thirty dollars. I went out to get Chinese food. When I came back Jamal's sister was pulling up. When I ran in the room to tell him, I caught sight of the girl's breasts bouncing. He was pulling her by the hair, telling her she was a good bitch.

He looked up at me. "Get out," he snapped.

"Okay," I said, "but Nancy's home."

Nancy was smart. She always obeyed her mom. We both knew she would tell. My uncle didn't care. He walked the girl right past his sister out the front door. When Nancy said she was going to tell, he responded: "Shut up, bitch."

My grandmother came home, and said the girl couldn't come back. Jamal ignored her. Day after day the girl returned. When this had been going on for over a month, Jamal showed me a slip of pink paper that showed she was pregnant.

"It's not mine," he snarled at her. "You're just trying to set me up." He grabbed her, and threw her out the window. It was only a five-foot drop. He went out, and started kicking her in the stomach.

I got outside, and pled with him. "Come on… stop."

"Naw," he grunted, kicking her again. "This slob bitch tried to set me up."

Our neighbors were watching, and getting more and more upset. He said: "You little niggas got it coming."

My Uncle Jamal started screaming. I pulled him away.

Finally his mom pulled into the driveway. She said to him, "You must be out your damn mind; you're no son of mine."

We went for the longest walk, not returning until that night. Nobody mentioned the incident. A couple of days later the girl returned with even more money, crying saying she was sorry. I didn't know what she was sorry for. We soon found out Johnny was in jail for attempted murder. That's why no one had seen him. All of this depressed Jamal, but there was nothing I could do or say.

When my mom moved us to Long Beach I was happy. She wanted us to think of ourselves as being different from her siblings. She put me in an alternative school connected to the mall. We took the public bus and trains everywhere, including school.

The school was like a huge office, with every grade in it. I noticed that my classmates segregated themselves by race and by hobby. There were skaters, blacks, and the Mexicans who were into graffiti. Everyone liked me because I ignored the segregation of the tables. I knew that the students felt comfortable around their own, so I worked to make them feel relaxed around me. I met a tall black guy named Jaquies who was about 16. He had long jheri curls. His gang was called "Insane gangster disciples" or "IGD." This confused me because it was so close to the name of an organization I already knew about. We became friends, and he taught me all about the street life of California. Jaquies got incarcerated every other week for doing what his big homies, or people in his gang, told him to do.

One day as we were walking he showed me a gun. He said he had just killed somebody in the alley. I didn't believe him at first, but as he told me the story, I had no choice. I was sure it was true. He started taking me around to his gang to buy weed. We both sold it at school. The girls we sold it to loved us. I dressed well and made them laugh, so they loved me even more.

These guys would kill anybody, even a member of their own gang, one they considered to be a brother. That made me nervous. Jaquies told me not to trust them. "Watch my back around those guys," he'd say. He was the kind of person that if you told him you didn't want to be his friend, he would kill you because you knew too much. He might not have been the worst. One of the guys already had a body count of eight people. I hated hearing about that, so I learned how to block out any information that would or could hurt me. I never repeated some of these things until now. I knew I wasn't where I wanted to be, and when Jaquies stopped coming to school, I felt relieved.

After one of my Mexican classmates got stabbed for talking to a girl in class, the kids at school seemed to think I was the man. My classmate talked to this girl who had a boyfriend who was in his thirties. He and a friend came to our school and stabbed my classmate to death. The clean-up crews got up the blood pretty fast in front of the main doors. We had to stay late for about an hour. The victim was a major fuck up, so people only talked about it for a week.

I did my work in class and excelled. The girls began to flock to my intelligent gangster personality. Our teacher never cared. I think she was afraid. One day while doing a project in class, I got to talking about sex. I think the girls knew I was a virgin, but they asked to see my dick. I showed them, bringing it out under the table. They looked, and laughed.

From their laughter, I assumed my seven inches must be incredibly small, but I didn't care. I was only twelve-and-a-half. I looked at the black girl on my left, and said it was her turn to show me something. She lifted her shirt. I waited for the right moment, when our teacher was distracted, and I began sucking the girl's firm nipple and breast. The Mexican girl on my right, Dominique, wanted to show me her pubic hair, but I wanted to see more. I asked to touch it. She let me rub her stomach right down to where her pubic hair started. Dominique had a boyfriend, so she wouldn't let me go further. I remembered what had happened to my Mexican classmate when he'd messed with the wrong girl. Still, I got money from those two girls. Sometimes they would walk me around the mall, talking about whatever, while I pretended to listen. I would let them spoil me.

The next week, as I was leaving to catch the bus, I tried to pick up what appeared to be grown woman. When I got on the bus the girl who'd let me suck on her breast laughed at me. According to her, the older girl I was trying to talk to was a man. I laughed too. It hadn't looked like a man. This person had boobs, a mini-skirt... all of it. The girl on the bus told me I'd been talking to a transsexual. There were a lot of them, she explained.

Dominique and I started talking. I asked her where she was going after school. She said she didn't want to go home, so she was visiting a friend. I told her she could go home with me, but she reminded me that she had a boyfriend. I explained that I didn't want to be her boyfriend. She thought about it, and agreed to come with me. At my house, I introduced her to my mom. We were allowed to play music in my room with the door open, so we listened to 2Pac.

The Doctor asked: "Were you and your mom finally getting along?"

"Somewhat," Daniel said.

Dominique came over a couple of times. My mom allowed that, but said that when she wasn't there, we couldn't go in my room. Dominique told me she was a Blood. She said the gangs had formed there in California to protect their members from the government, and from anyone who wanted to hurt them. Her father had taught her how the government had brought drugs to black people to poison them. They felt black people were becoming a threat. She said the Bloods had once been organized to help kids. They did, but there wasn't enough money to do much.

Dominique told me that there had been a time when black people could only get houses in certain neighborhoods. The Bloods wanted to protect the only thing they had, which was 'hoods like Compton. That was why 'hoods like Compton were full of Bloods.

I told her she didn't know what she was talking about, and punched her, playfully. She punched me, and I kissed her. We walked outside under the carport. When I rubbed my hands between her legs, we agreed to be fuck friends, but we wouldn't let it interfere with our friendship. When she told me she'll kill for me, I began falling in love.

A few days later, I called her, and she came over. I was planning to have sex for the first time. As we sat on the couch kissing, my mother walked in. My mother greeted Dominique, then went into the kitchen, and back to her room. She came out a few minutes later, saying "I don't have time for this." She looked at Dominique and said, "You have to leave."

When I asked her what she was talking about, she decided I was talking back to her. I wished I had my marble.

Dominique had left. I headed to the door to catch her on the way to the bus stop. I couldn't find Dominique, so I went to the park. I put my shades upside down on my face, and thought about everything that just happened. Where was my marble? Was it still under the floorboard where I'd left it? An old man approached me. He claimed to be with the Mexican mafia. He tried to order me to kill someone, telling me how to do it. He promised he would reward me with great power. He left a knife by my side, and walked away.

I took off as fast as I could. As soon as I reached the entrance the cops came out. They threw me against a window, as if I were a grown man. They wouldn't tell me what I'd done wrong. They took me in, and put me in a cell. I waited to find out what the charge was. Three months later I Finally learned I'd been brought in for violating my probation.

They gave me a year in jail. While I was in there, my cellmate went on about a guy who was going to stab me for rank. He said me he would help me, and for some reason I believed him. As the door opened for us to go to the bathroom, he told me to go. I rushed out and beat the guy senseless, as guards yelled: "OC warning! OC Warning!" They subdued me, and put me in a cold basement cell with very little light. That cell was all I knew for two weeks. The walls started to close in on me. I boxed against my shadow on the wall. I made shapes out of wet toilet tissue. I did anything I could to hold on to my sanity. I needed my marble.

When they released me from the hole, the guy I'd beaten came asking for my forgiveness. He wanted to know what he'd done to make me mad. I told him what my cellmate had said. He said that he and my cellmate had issues, and my cellmate had set me up for the fall. I was starting to think this was the worst place I'd ever been. I could not understand Spanish, but the Mexican gangs were watching me.

I needed protection, so I had to get into a gang. I connected with 74 IGD (Insane gangster disciples). He and a Hoover Crip had killed most of a family. They'd killed the mother and daughter. The son was in jail with us, but they wanted him dead too. Killing him would be my way into the gang. I did not want to do it. Killing this guy, and entering another gang, would betray my organization. I thought about escape, but it was clear the guards would kill us. You could get a year just for talking about escape. I wondered why these gang members wanted this guy dead. Obviously he hadn't told on them. They had already killed his family.

As we are talking, the guy walked by. The gang's leader soldier was doing pull ups on the monkey bars. The lead soldier threatened the guy, making a slashing motion across his throat. There in the gym these guys told me what to do. I said no, realizing this put me in trouble. But for some reason I never saw them again.

After twelve months in that place, I knew it was as close to prison as I ever wanted to be. When I was released my probation officer picked me up and told me I was no longer on probation. She took me to her office in Los Angeles where my mom met us. I was upset with my mom. I wanted to tell her how I felt. I thought she'd abandoned me. I wanted to tell her how alone I'd felt, and how I'd given up on my life. Instead I said nothing, and held in my feelings.

As we arrived at my grandmother's house, I began putting things together. That's when I realized that my mom had been the one who had locked me up. She'd done it because she could not take care of me.

At my grandmother's house my mom and my sisters had their own room. That first night my Uncle Jamal and I got drunk, and smoked a lot of weed. We got a good price on some wet sticky weed that was not at all average. My uncle insisted that I smoke it. As I did, he started telling me how he believed the guy who just sold us this weed might've put embalming fluid on it. My older Uncle Johnny had smoked weed like this, and the first time he'd done it, he'd tried to kill one of his sisters. "This is shirm," we both said out loud, but it was too late. We had already smoked it. "Shirm" is what we called PCP. We sat in the car with the widows up. Jamal said the guy who'd sold us the weed, had caught him sleeping with his wife. We had to confront this guy, said Jamal. So at three-in-the-morning, before I'd been free for even 24 hours, there I was, grabbing a knife from the kitchen. Nobody fucked with me, or my family. Nobody could get away with poisoning us. If need be, this guy would die.

I put on my uncle's blue dickey pants and blue all-star shoes with their tongues flipped back. I wore a white tee shirt. As we walked down the street, I did the C rip walk my uncle had taught me, throwing up gang signs, and disrespecting everybody. We walked up to the second floor apartment where the guy lived. His ugly wife answered the door. What teeth she had were crooked. I didn't care. My uncle said he wanted her to suck his dick.

Eventually we found the guy. When he got in my uncle's face, I threw him over the rail. We laughed and walked downstairs to the garages. There we kept on beating him. His wife begged us to stop, but to me that meant nothing. As I stomped him over and over, I thought he was going to die. Then I started kicking at his teeth. As I choked him, he slobbered and scratched at me. I choked him harder, until he went limp. That's when my uncle pulled me off of him. We went home, grabbed some beer, and I bragged about the blood on my shoes. My uncle felt we should've done more, so at five that morning we broke into his garage where we stole everything we could find.

"Now you said earlier that jail was as close to prison as you wanted to be, that you never wanted to return. So why, within the first 24 hours of being out, would you risk going back?" The Doctor asked with a suspicious smirk.

"It was the only life I knew," said Daniel. "I wasn't concerned about jail, just respect. Respect was the only thing that kept me going in jail."

I was walking on air that day. When we got home, I slept the entire day. None of the little kids in the neighborhood would fuck with us now, but there was a guy named Poncho, a big-time Blood known for killing people. Now he wanted a piece of us. One day he almost got us in front of a store. I remember him saying: "Come here, bro." In California bloods say "bro" for "Blood".

"He's going to kill us," said my uncle, so we dropped my blue beach cruiser, and ran as fast as the wind. I got to the roof of a two-story apartment building, and went home from there. By that time my mom had seen enough. I'd barely been out for two weeks when we were on the road again.

The Doctor looks at his watch.

"I know, doc. It's time for me to go back. I hand him the marble.

Now I mostly eat and study. Each day I get an hour-long workout at the hospital gym. Though it seems like weeks, it's only days before I see the Doctor again.

CHAPTER 10

We moved back to Daphne, Alabama, where from day one I began to lose my mind. I remembered that I had put my marble in the closet at the Big House, and the peace it brought me. The first chance I got I retrieved it.

We moved back into the old rundown trailer behind the Big House. They still had my dog, Destiny, but her name was now Daphne. She looked depressed and starved, and walked around confused. My cousin said that she'd bit several of them, and had eaten three of her own babies. She was happy to see me, but I could tell something had changed. Eventually she would disappear forever.

The trailer looked worse than it had. The floorboards were rotting, and it smelled of mildew. Rats, snakes and flying cockroaches were regular visitors. Keeping our possessions clean was a constant chore. Every day we cleaned, and we always kept the grass mowed short.

One day my mom told me to cut our half of the grass. As I was cutting it, Bill told me to cut the Big House grass on the side and in front. He refused to let me use the riding mower. Instead I had a push mower that cut off every ten seconds. It wasn't easy in the heat. All those things upset me. As I mowed, I thought about the fact that we were living outside of the Big House so we wouldn't have to listen to all that they said. I kept cutting our part of the lawn, but I didn't cut any of theirs.

That's when Bill came out and beat me with a stick. When I told my mom what he'd done, she did nothing. I started to feel like everything was my fault. My mom said that I was responsible for raising my two sisters, but they didn't seem to know that.

While babysitting one day, I told my youngest sister, I was going to hang her by her shirt on the gate. Though I'd only meant it as a joke, she begged me to actually do it. I did, and there she was, swinging. Her older sister, saw this, and she wanted to swing. I put her up there. When I let them down, she got angry, saying I took too long to get her down off the fence.

She went to our mom, pulling on her shirt in a choking motion, and saying: "Daniel hung us on the gate like this." Our mom made me get in the bathtub, where she beat me with an extension cord. Once I escaped, I ran from the trailer, heading for the woods. There I found the old fig tree where I felt safe. As I ran I yelled to my mom that I hated her. I said I wanted to go live with my dad. I hadn't even seen him since I was seven.

As I sat underneath the fig tree, playing with my marble I wondered where my friend was. I begin to call out for him. "Hey, where are you?" I called. I heard no answer, and thought I was alone. I looked into my marble, and mumbled, "You said you would show me a better place." Tears formed in my eyes. I trembled. With each breath I grew weaker. My marble started to change. Within it I could see spirals of yellow, blue, green, and orange. Suddenly I was overwhelmed with joy, happiness, and peace. I was becoming one with nature. And there, surrounded in a warm glow, still youthful, was my friend.

"Where have you been?" I sobbed.

"With you," he said.

"How could you be with me? I never saw you," I said as I stood up.

"Did you believe that I was there?" he asked, coming closer.

"No!"

"I have always been there," he said softly, reaching for my marble.

We walked through woods, and I found myself entering the vortex of colors I'd seen in a dream. Now I wanted to see it. I was no longer afraid.

"Where are we going?" I asked.

"To the place that you seek" he said.

"Where is that?" I asked.

"Halisaseas!" he exclaimed.

"Halisaseas?" I repeated.

"Yes", he said.

As we continued, I noticed the leaves on the trees turning money green. My eyes widened, and filled with greed. The red-breasted robins in the trees chirped in a seductive harmony, almost like the singing of a beautiful girl. My heart filled with lust. The sky was a deep blue, reminding me of the respect that I had gained from my uncles. I felt myself filling with pride.

"How much longer?" I pleaded.

He abruptly turned toward me. "You are not ready yet," he announced. "You have been bitten by a snake and the poison runs through your veins. Be cautious of the snakes that lurk in the shadows. Take this marble, and return from whence you came."

"I want to go to Halisaseas," I protested. Before I could finish my sentence he was gone. There I was, back in the cold cruel world, standing beneath the fig tree. I felt miserable as I went back home to my mother.

Most days my mother and I said very little to one another. Then one day, as she dumped boric acid around the trailer she said: "Any guy can make a baby but it takes a man to raise one."

"Funny,' I said. "I thought that I applied to women too."

She looked at me. "I did the best I could, but I can't show you how to be a man."

A week later she sent me to Atlanta to live with my dad, however she didn't tell him I was coming. When I got off the bus I called him, asking if he could come get me.

"Where are you?" he asked.

"I'm here in Atlanta, at the bus station."

"Right there at the bus station? I can't believe it. You hold on. I'll be there," he promised. It was a couple of hours before he showed up.

He had a girlfriend, Angela. She looked like Gina in the TV show, *Martin*—very attractive, but she didn't seem to like me. Angela had a small boy of her own, and she seemed to want my father to be his father. I guess she thought my father's relationship with me was a threat. Having me there complicated my dad's method of making money. At the time he was selling weed.

He called my mom, wanting her to take me back, but he could not reach her. When she didn't return his calls, he sent me to live with his mom in Mobile. Though his mom didn't like my mom, she tried not to talk trash about her, but every now and again a few things slipped out. When we all went down there, Angela and my father stayed for a couple of days. Around that time they started arguing. I didn't know what their problem was, but I could feel the intensity building. I thought maybe he'd cheated on Angela with her sister. Whatever it was, Angela was going to make him feel her pain. Even at 13 I recognized that. I could feel her vindictiveness. Yet I also knew my father would kill her if she cheated on him.

After my father left, I listened to Angela cry in the living room. She was building up her rage, getting ready to release her inner fire. She was like a female dragon protecting its weakest spot. She would use the strongest defense she had: her hot womb.

Angela came in the room where I was lying in my dad's brother's bed. Wearing black lingerie, she curled up beside me. When she scooted her butt closer to my butt, I got an erection. I rolled over and faced her. I felt as if I was going to cum in my pants. Something stirred in my stomach, and my penis got so hard it hurt. I put my arm around her and held her. I didn't know what was happening. When I looked up my dad was watching through the door hinges. His piercing eyes caught mine. She saw him and got up. A few days later my father left me there with his mom. He didn't explain why, but I had my suspicions.

The Doctor asks, "Daniel, how did you feel seeing your dad, and experiencing this?"

"Well, I was happy and confused at the same time," Daniel replies. "I thought maybe someone was testing me, that maybe she wanted my father to choose between me and her. Still I had a grown woman in the bed with me, and could not control my desire. I also felt like it was my fault for a while, then his fault because he did choose her over me."

I turned to the local Organization again. They tied a bandana around my eyes, blindfolding me. They beat me with a black flag for minutes. Then they invited me to a party. I went, taking two shotguns from my grandmother's house. I hid these in my pants leg. At the party we shot, drank and smoked weed. When I was walking home I got ambushed. They took my pants and guns. One guy put a .32 pistol to my head.

"I'm going to kill this fucker," he said.

Just as he started to squeeze the trigger, one of his friends screamed: "No!" and snatched his arm. This friend told me to go home.

When I told my grandmother what had happened, she called my dad. He came down from Atlanta the next day. He found the guys, but they told him I'd sold them the guns. He believed them. He didn't ask them how much they paid me, or wonder why I didn't have any money. If I'd had some money, I would have run to California. I had a feeling my mom was back there again.

My grandmother and dad decided I should go back, and stay at the Big House. Some of the family were there from California, including my uncle Jamal. I stayed there for a weekend. Jamal and I ordered pizza, and reminisced about getting into trouble. When he ate over half of an extra large pizza I told him I think he'd smoked too much pot. Though he hadn't smoked for hours, he still acted high.

My first day there was okay. As Jamal and I walked through the woods I told him how sometimes I heard voices and saw people who weren't physically there. Though he laughed at me, I wasn't offended. I told him about my troubles with Bill, and how I felt as if I were living in hell. My Uncle Jamal said: "I feel bad for you. I was going to bring you a gun—a

Glock 9—but I didn't think I could get it onto the airplane. It might've worked though. The gun's mostly plastic."

I shook my head. "I'm pretty sure it's got some metal parts in it, so you probably would've had trouble. I'm glad you didn't try."

He went on about his own problems, and about how he'd tried to commit suicide with pills. Finally we found some pot and smoked it. We passed out downstairs listening to Kurt Cobain, a musician who'd committed suicide.

The next morning Bill woke up and told me to wash the dishes. He said I should finish cleaning out the trailer, and then I should cut the grass.

"No," I said. "I don't live here."

When he grabbed me and slapped me, my uncle said: "I dare you to try that shit on me."

Bill obliged. Jamal tried to fight back, but Bill was too big. Jamal tried to run. Bill threw an axe at Jamal's feet, barely missing him. Jamal started crying. He picked up a rock the size of a baseball, and glanced at me. I looked at my marble. It was red. I gave him the okay. Jamal tossed the rock through the driver side widow of Bill's Porsche. As Bill started chasing us, adrenalin pumped through our veins.

We headed into the woods. We planned to hide out there, but Jamal lived in California, and I couldn't even get myself to my dad's mom house. When Jamal started getting hysterical, I told him I wanted to show him a place called Halisaseas. We walked through the woods, searching, but I couldn't find the fig tree. I shut up about the whole thing, resolving not to tell him more without evidence. I did show him the marble, but to him it was just a normal marble.

I told Jamal it would be okay, and I would take the beating. I didn't describe what Bill was going to do to me. I was hoping Bill would take his anger out on me. I was used to his beatings. His violence and sexual abuse just made me stronger. I went in. When Bill started I dashed toward the woods, but he caught me hard with the switches.

I'd been taking beatings from tied switches all my life, so this was nothing new to me. Terrance and some others were waiting to stop me at the tree line. Terrance grabbed me, and made a half-hearted effort to hold me. "You just have to face him," he said.

I turned, and there was Bill, the size of a bear. He ran right up and punched me in the face over and over. I went numb. Though he was punching me hard, I thought of him as weak. I cried inside, but not outside. Blood welled up in my mouth. "Where's your uncle?" he repeated over and over. I told him nothing. Instead I thought of how they'd tortured Jesus

Christ. The most he could do was kill me.

Later they took me to my dad's mom's house. I was afraid of what might have happened to Jamal. He called a week later. After I'd left they'd come to the tree line, and told him to get in the car for the airport, but his mother turned the car around and took him back to the Big House. Bill dragged him from the car, kicking and beating him. "Everywhere," I asked, thinking of his face.

"Everywhere," he repeated. After I hung up, I cried. This is what they'd done to Sydney.

I didn't tell my dad what happened. He took me back to Georgia, but he and his girlfriend treated me like crap. He bought me a radio, and designer clothes, but these meant nothing. He didn't spend time with me.

I turned to gangs. When a boy on the bus talked about my gang, I beat him up, and got suspended from school. My dad was angry. That night I went outside and wished on a star. I asked for a better life, and a family of my own, so I could raise a child the way I wished I could've been raised.

The next day I returned to school. I was waiting at the bus stop, when the guy I'd assaulted on the bus ran towards me waving a butcher knife tied to the end of a broomstick. He sliced my windbreaker. When I looked on the ground I saw that the blade had bent, so I beat him up again.

The convenience store clerk complained when I smeared the guy's blood on his car. He called the Norfolk police. I was expelled from school. My dad beat me and threatened to shoot me. I was getting him way too much attention. So I ran away.

I didn't eat anything for three days. I met a Mexican guy, and started breaking into cars with him. We got everything from sex toys to money. One night at the hotel I broke into twenty-three cars. My Mexican friend's family fed me, but they didn't allow me to spend the night in the house. Instead I slept in the woods. Out there alone, for the first time I felt completely safe. I awoke, surrounded by water from the rain.

I could not take this life. I could not keep hurting hardworking people. The whole thing was starting to bother me. I turned myself in. They tried to find my dad, but couldn't, so I became a ward of the state. They put me in a detention center with adults for a few months. One guy hated my name and tried to get me to wipe his ass. I politely declined, I knew I was going to die and no one would care. Suffering became a way of life.

Another guy in the detention center had charges ranging from robbery to murder. He was going to prison. When he became my friend, I found out he was a Muslim. When he found out what my cellmate was trying to do to me, he beat him halfway to death.

A week later I was watching TV in the rec room when a guy said my name. When I turned around, I saw a skinny black guy. He said: "Remember? I tried to stab you."

"Yeah," I said. "What's up, man?"

He said he was sorry, and that he'd been on crack. He was only about 13, and I knew it could've been me. He said he'd brought his father's gun to school, but I wasn't there anymore. "I was going to kill you," he said. "I'm sorry."

I told him I was sorry too, and that was that.

From there I was sent to live with a family in Buford, Georgia, outside of Savannah. It was okay, but it was more like a foster home. The government paid this family to take care of me, but the parents spent most of it on their own kids. Clothes, and other things that were supposed to be for me, went to their kids.

I turned to gangs again, and I hung out at an apartment where most of my gang friends lived. One day while talking crap outside, I looked up to see a light-skinned black girl in the window. Out of nowhere I said to her: "You want to have some fun?" She invited me in. That made the guys jealous, and they followed me.

"Get the fuck away from my door," she told them. I went in, and within an hour the girl and I were having sex. We kept doing this for the next month. Sometimes she wanted it nine times in a day, and I just kept going through the motions, as if I were cumming.

When I got tired of her, I told her she had to fuck anybody in my gang anytime they wanted. She did what I told her to do. One of the other gang members fell in love with her, and asked her out. When I found out I started punching and kicking him. He wouldn't stop moving, so I kept beating him. Finally I dragged his body into the road. A grown man ran out and saw what was happening. I yelled at him, saying he should come out there, and I'd give him the same treatment. He ran away and called the police. When they came I beat one of them, then one of them hit me over the head. I awakened with my legs crossed and bound. I found myself in a chokehold, and started foaming at the mouth.

I got charged with twelve counts of assault and battery. The public defender argued that the cops had used a restraint technique that was not permitted. They agreed to let me plead guilty to two counts of assault, and they would drop everything else. I was sentenced to serve six months in Decatur, Georgia. All I remember about that place was that the guys were big, and I had to fight every single day. They were the sharks and I was the fresh fish. If any of them asked for my food, I had to give it to them, or fight. I even fought when I was eating. It would happen at breakfast, then we'd go back to our cells. The guys would say they were going to see me at lunchtime. The fight continued then, and every day. It was a way of life. I was glad to be released from that place. They gave me back my possessions, including my marble.

THIS PAGE LEFT INTENTIONALLY BLANK

CHAPTER 11

My mother picked me up from Decatur. I moved back into the Big House, and never saw my father again. I missed him, but I'd heard he'd gotten a 40-year prison sentence for murder and drug trafficking.

Often I tried to do the right thing, but it was too late for me to change. No matter what happened, whether at home or at school, it was always my fault. My cousin Terrance in Alabama tried to help me stay out of fights, but, for some reason, the gangs around there wanted a piece of me. One day, when I was walking the streets, a gray car drove past. I noticed the driver was a guy I'd fought a long time ago. The car made a quick U-turn, and the driver stuck his hand out the window. I started walking quickly away, but as soon I turned I heard gunshots. I ran and jumped a fence. A piece of the fence went straight through my hand, but I was too excited to notice. As I neared home, my mom heard a thunderous noise. When I got there she saw my bleeding hand, and figured I'd been hit there. Once I got a couple of stitches I was ok. After that I couldn't stay out of trouble. I'd thought of school as a place where I could escape the problems of home, but even there I wasn't safe.

I met new people in science class. My teacher teamed me with two other students to do a science project. Before this I had rarely associated with people of other races who weren't criminals. This was especially true of white people. My family had always told me white people were out to get black people. They wanted all of us in jail, they said. "Don't you go to school, putting them white people in our business," they'd say. Sometimes they'd add: "Once those white people get you, they won't let you go." This got me scared. I resented all people outside my race. When my family talked about the "house nigger" they meant someone who turned in other black people, or helped white people keep them in jail. A black cop in the south might've been seen this way.

One of my team members was a foreigner and the other one was a white girl. I went to the white girl's house in the Lake Forest suburb around the corner from where I lived. Her parents were very hospitable. They let us stay upstairs and study with the door closed. I felt scared and confused. If anything went wrong, I knew I would get the blame. I was the poor black boy who always got into trouble. Secretly I wished we'd kept the door open, just to be on the safe side. But even when the girl's mom brought us milk and cookies, she closed the door when she left. My marble was always blue. I pulled it out and held it whenever I needed to feel calm.

I never tried to do anything bad with that girl; we really did study. The next day I made a 90 on my test and a 100 on our science project. It was the first time I had done so well. One day my marble turned a purplish color and stayed that way for days. I tried to make new friends of other races so I could get a different perspective on life; I even tried to embrace my spirituality. But I could not stay out of trouble.

My new white friends just wanted weed, and I couldn't understand what my foreign friends were talking about. Soon I had to get back on the streets, just to find people I could relate to. My marble changed, going back to primary colors. Something was different in me too; I craved insight but didn't know how to get it. I began going through emotional changes.

I was scared. Many nights I would lie in bed unable to move. I knew where I was but I literally could not lift a finger. When I told people about this, they said the devil was riding my back. I learned to conquer this by saying: "I reedbuck you in the name of Jesus." Saying it always worked, so I knew God was real. This wasn't the first or last time I saw or heard strange things.

One day I saw what appeared to be an owl the size of a man sitting in a tree staring at me. At first I wasn't sure what I was looking at, then as I walked closer to the tree, its head turned unnaturally, so much so that nothing could explain it. The huge creature opened its wings, turned its head all the way around, and soared into the sky. It blocked out part of the moon. This gave me the feeling that the devil was on me, and he was not finished tempting me.

I slept in a room, about as big as a walk-in closet, where my great-grandmother had slept. Every so often, I could see a white light, but it seemed to come from nowhere. I never approached it; I just put my head under the pillow and went back to sleep. I wondered what would happen if I just went into the light. Would my great-grandmother be waiting there for me to take me out of this crazy world? My cousin Bryan had told me a little about our family. He said that angels were always watching us. Our great-grandmother had been a full-blooded Indian, Bryan told me. She'd had special powers, and now I lay in her room with all of her belongings.

I could hear her rocking chair sometimes, even though there wasn't one in the room. I knew it was her spirit, but that never caused me any bad feelings. I never felt I had to cry, or run away. Most people are scared of the unknown. I was more inquisitive than frightened. I wanted to know what was on the other side. I was no longer afraid of death; I just didn't want to die alone.

Around this time the girls at school became interested in me. I learned a lot In just two weeks. I got two girls to pick me up from the Big House, and went to their house. I could only get one to have sex with me. The other girl was afraid. I came home feeling relaxed, but soon I needed more. I felt as if my new influences gave me power, the same kind of power Bryan had. I'd learned that if I was honest with girls they'd be more likely to give me what I wanted. If I did that, nobody's feelings would be hurt.

The first girls were kind of big, and I wanted to see more. Terrance and I went to his friend's house to see them. I had them naked within an hour. I sent Terrance to the back while I watched the girls make out. I was too drunk to have sex, so it was just entertainment.

My last and hardest challenge was approaching. My marble stayed a constant yellow. I noticed a white girl in the library who had nothing in common with me. I wanted to prove my theory about girls respecting honesty, and if I could get with her, that would do it. One day I sat down across from her and glanced under the table. She had nice legs, and wore cowboy boots. I followed her unblemished legs up to her sundress. She had nice boobs that stuck out beneath her dress. I figure she had to be at least sixteen. I asked her name, and she said it was Kaley.

"That's a pretty name," I said. "My name's Daniel. You should understand this about me: I'm not looking for any long-term relationship, but if you want to give me a chance, I'll be your friend."

"What kind of friend?" she asked.

"The kind of friend who'll fuck you so hard, you won't be able to stand afterwards. I know all about satisfying a woman," I said, smelling the scents of ocean and flowers in her hair. Her scent aroused me. I looked down at her and said: "I'm sorry for my bizarre behavior. I'm bedazzled by your beauty." I got up, and walked back to my table, my hard cock sticking out from my paints for all to see. When her class hour was up in the library, she walked by and handed me her number. I thought it was fake because I knew this attractive white girl was out of my league.

I was impatient to get home that day. When I got in, I went upstairs, called her, and told her I wanted to come over. She told me I had to make it quick. I had Terrance take me over there. When I first saw her again, she was even more beautiful than before. I stood by the door and chatted for a minute. I'd always been told that white people didn't like black people, but I could tell from her brother this wasn't true. He was cool as hell. He kept passing by the door, making comments, and telling me what was up. He seemed like your stereotypical black kid.

Terrance began to rush me. I thought he was jealous. I asked Kaley if I could come back later.

"Okay," she agreed. "Come back tonight, and bring some weed."

I went home and imagined what I was going to do to her. She had strong, smooth thighs, and a smile that made me forget about my troubled life. I went out looking for weed, and it took all day to find it. Because I'd been out all day, I wasn't allowed to go out that night. I could sneak out, but then I'd need a ride. I never called her, because my embarrassment trumped the truth. Here I was, a gangster, but I couldn't even get over there. I should have told her the truth, but I doubted that she would appreciate it. That ruined my theory.

That Sunday morning I woke up to the smell of bacon and eggs. I was really tired from smoking weed and drinking the night before. I opened my eyes and sat up.

"Come downstairs and get washed up," my aunt called to me.

As I slowly regained consciousness, I slid my cold feet into my warm black house shoes. I braced myself with the bed, then started hobbling on my own. I started slowly down the stairs. My procrastination was interrupted by my aunt's shout: "You better be ready for church!"

I started to turn around to go back upstairs, then I realized, *I'm already thirteen going on fourteen*. A long time before, in California, my mother had told me: "When you turn thirteen you can decide what religion you want to practice, but until then your actions are my responsibility".

Remembering this conversation, I continued down the stairs. I knew that my mom would have my back, so I stood tall, ready to finally face my aunt. I practiced what I would say. It would be this: "I'm not going to church today; I'm a, Muslim, I'll be upstairs asleep."

As I approached the arched French doorway to the living room, I could see directly into the kitchen. I met her eyes. She stood, her index finger pointing me back toward the stairs. I froze.

"Get ready for church before I beat your damn ass!" she snapped. She turned, mumbling: "Making me swear on Sunday…"

She was about five feet tall and could barely walk. I knew I could take her. But then I realized what had happened to Sydney when he'd tried to stand alone. I walked back upstairs. For a while I sat on the edge of my bed, grasping my marble, and mumbling, "I ain't got to take this shit."

Someone must've heard my smart comments. My aunt started telling my mom how hardheaded I was. She said they should do something about me. Then I could hear my cousin, Brandy's voice: "No, he just needs a good ass-whipping."

Brandy was about twenty-seven, and had always been dependent on her mother and father. I thought: *How dare you try to raise me!* Brandy had a son who called her names like "stranger." Suddenly it felt as if someone were shining a powerful, hot light in my face. My eyes burned, then it went black. As light returned, I realized my head was bouncing off the bed. I slid to the floor.

"Get dressed," a deep voice said. It was my 270-pound Uncle Bill. He'd done this before. I got up off the floor and tried to follow him, gripping the doorframe. My mom stood at the bottom off the stairs. She looked sad, but I didn't need her pity.

"Fuck you," I said. "I hope you all die, I'm not going to church. On my G's, if you touch me I'll kill you, motherfucker." My voice rose to a scream. I cried.

Bill started back at me, but my aunt grabbed his hand. Then she looked at me, and said: "You wait till we get back.

I should've been afraid, but a plot emerged from my thoughts. I grabbed my marble. It turned red, and was hot to the touch.

THIS PAGE LEFT INTENTIONALLY BLANK

CHAPTER 12

I sat up on the bed and the pain began to set in. My face throbbed, but that went away, as I clinched my fist and exhaled deeply. I thought to myself: *If I burn the house down, they would have no place to live. Then they would feel my emptiness. They would stop worrying about troubling me because they would have bigger things to worry about.* All of a sudden those thoughts stopped. I realized that they would know it was me. I was only thirteen. If I just ran away how I would survive? I really had enjoyed the time I'd spent incarcerated. Most of my friends were in there, and they respected me. Also, I hadn't done so badly in Ohio, and I'd never been incarcerated there. My friend, Bryan lived the street life, and was really on his own. I was sure he could help me survive until I was eighteen. I could imagine sleeping from house to house, staying with different women every night, drinking. No one would judge me there.

I knew how I would do it. I would take a car, and all the money I could find. When I ran out of money, I'd start robbing people. *What's the worst that could happen?* I thought. Most of the people I'd been locked up with had committed serious crimes, but they'd be released when they turned eighteen or twenty-one.

So the Doctor asked, "Daniel, were you planning on being locked up?"

"No but I expected it, and I didn't care either way." Daniel could feel the warmth of the marble in his pocket, as he continued the story.

I lay on the bed and waited for them to leave. It seemed like forever, "What the fuck are they doing?" I asked myself. Then I rolled over and slid down to the bottom of the bed. I tiptoed to the top of the stairs to see if I could hear anything. It was completely quiet. My heart beat faster and the adrenalin rush got stronger. I went back to the room and paced back and forth. I said to myself, "I'm ready, I'm ready…" over and over and then I sprinted down the stairs, passed the front door, ran through the living room, next the family room, finally the kitchen. I stopped and noticed an empty wooden key holder. Where the hell were the keys? I started looking for money. Everybody's room was locked except for Grandpa's. I opened his drawer, but found nothing except thermal underclothes. There was a stale smell. I noticed a fanypack's waist strap hanging from underneath the pillow. I opened it and pulled out a black .22 pistol. "Okay, this is a start," I said to myself. "Now I can get a car and some money." After gently slipping the pistol back into place, I walked upstairs.

I knew I had to get hyped. No more thinking about it! I would do what needed to be done! I no longer controlled my actions; I grabbed my black overall dickeys and some black chucks. I was petrified. I had no sense of time, and I didn't know how long they'd been gone. I dressed quickly, grabbed my marble, and headed downstairs to the kitchen. On the way to the kitchen I remembered that Bill had a bigger gun on the wall in his room. When I was in jail I'd learned that if I used a gun to commit a crime, the owner could be liable. That would be great! I hated Bill! But his door was locked. I really wanted to get in.

I knew that I could break in anywhere. First I went outside and tried Bill's bedroom window. I opened it and climbed in. There it was. I smiled. The magazine and the shape of the gun told me it was an Uzi, like in the movies. I took it off the wall, placing the strap across my shoulders.

I headed back towards the window when it dawned on me: *This gun is entirely too big.* I would get arrested before I got a block away. Looking to my left I noticed a wardrobe closet. It had a vintage look and it was huge. Rifling through his old bellbottom polyester pants, I grabbed a black trench coat. I stuck my head out the window to make sure no one was watching. The coast was clear, I started to walk down the long hilly road leading from the house. As I walked, I began to sweat. My eyes burned and I tasted salt in my mouth.

Not too many cars came down our road, but we knew everyone who did. I realized I had to get off the road. I cut through the woods. The heat was becoming unbearable. Taking off the coat and the strap at the same time, I held the weapon closely, as if it were a child needing protection. I saw a white building about a half of football field away—a church. I walked around it. Once I got to a gas station I used the pay phone.

The first person I thought about was a guy that I knew from school; a small, skinny white boy who wanted to be a gangster. He was too soft for most of my plan, but at that moment he would be useful. There were boys like him in jail who were killers, but not him. All I needed him for was transportation. I laid the balled up coat in the phone booth. I picked up the receiver with the sleeve of the coat. I had a small black box about the size of a cigarette box. It was a device to send out tones corresponding to those in a dialed phone number. I could place the box next to the phone, it would play the number, and, just like that, the phone on the other end would start to ring.

I called the guy and asked him to come and pick me up. With no questions he replied "I'll be there in a minute." Needing a place to lay low I walked to the side of the building. Waiting there I heard a voice inside my head: "It's not too late, Daniel. Turn back; you could even sneak in the window, just fight back." I disregarded the thoughts. These were weak emotions that would only get me hurt. I couldn't afford to be afraid.

The guy I called (we will refer to him as "Chris") pulled up in a small tricked out Honda Accord with small rims, and lights flashing underneath. As I headed to the passenger door I knew my poor planning would turn out badly, but I got in anyway. Chris had no idea what I was up to.

"Where do you want to go?" Chris asked.

I showed him the weapon and told him: "Anywhere. I'm having a bad day."

He simply said, "Okay," and put on some music. I laid my head back and let go of reality. I daydreamed about my cousins and I, all drinking, and smoking the biggest blunts (marijuana rolled in a cigar) you ever saw. We had the most gorgeous women in the world and the nicest cars ever. No one told us what to do. We ran the streets, and would die for it anytime.

My daydreaming was interrupted. Chris was saying he would be right back. I looked around. We'd stopped at a beautiful two-story house. Even the grass didn't look real. I thought to myself that this was the house I should be robbing. I got impatient. I felt like a sitting duck in the car with that weapon.

Just then a figure appeared in a doorway on the side of the house. A soft female voice whispered, "Hey! Come in." I was reluctant at first, but her voice calmed me down. She sounded so kind. I couldn't help myself. I opened the car door, followed her scent of sweet candy and roses, and got to the entrance to the house. She held the screen door open for me. She had a natural tan with blondish hair and highlights.

As I walked by my arm brushed her hand. A jolt of electricity raised the hair on my arm. That split second felt like minutes. I wanted it to last for hours. I burned her image into my head as she closed the door. Her brown eyes and lustful lips were welcoming. I sat in the chair closest to the door.   "Hi. I'm Amanda," she said. "Chris is in the bathroom. Would you like something to drink?"

"Yes," I said.

"Alabama is hot," she said, turning towards the kitchen.

From the corner of my eye I watched her long legs as she walked. I felt guilty, and realized she might be the last girl I would see. I watched more closely as she opened the refrigerator door. I visualized her curves all the way up the back of her legs to the center of her back. Then finally there it was. *For a white girl she's got an ass,* I thought to myself.

Amanda brought me the drink in a can. I laid the coat on the floor. She pulled the cap back and the liquid instantly started to spill over.

"I'm sorry," she cried, then she ran back to the kitchen, grabbed paper towels, came back, and knelt at my feet. I felt so powerful. Her 17-year-old boobs shook in her low white halter top. They squeezed together, and I imagined my cock wedged between them. As she stood up, the bottom of her yellow flowered skirt lagged behind.

She knew I was looking as she folded the lagging skirt with her hand. As she stood in front of me, her flat stomach with its pierced navel ring was at eye level. I asked: "Do you want me to move so you can get this here." I pointed at the wet spot on the side of my thigh.

"No," she replied, giggling. She bent over and started wiping my leg.

This is it, I thought. I wondered if she knew that Chris was a punk, and wouldn't do anything if she made out with me.

She stepped on the coat on the floor. "What's that?" she asked, feeling the huge bulge.

"My Uzi," I replied.

She smiled, walked away, and threw the used paper towels in the trash.

I could hear her mumbling in the hallway. I looked around for a split second and thought about what I could steal. Then I thought that she was a very nice person, so I shouldn't steal from her. I continued to wait.

Amanda came back with a huge smile on her face and plopped down beside me.

"Let me see it," she said.

"What?" I asked.

"Your gun."

I jokingly reached for my zipper, and glanced at her. There was no change in her expression. She was still smiling at me.

Feeling like I had pushed the limit, I pulled out the gun. She ran her fingertip along the side, making sure never to grab it out my hand. Then she looked up and said: "I like it."

I placed my hand on her thigh. "Is he still in the bathroom?"

"Yes," she replied.

I was so new at this. I kept my hand on that one spot on her leg forever. This seemed like my last shot. I leaned over and asked her to come closer. She asked why. I told her I would tell her a secret. As she leaned toward me, I started telling her how I was going to rob a bank when I left. "I'll be rich," I said. The entire time I was sliding my hand closer and closer to her hidden treasure.

She responded with deep sighs. I brushed my lips against her cheeks, and went for it. My hand was there. I could feel her wet lips between my fingers. Then: "Whoosh!" It was the fucking toilet flushing. She sat up quickly, fixing her panties. It took about two minutes before the door opened. Chris was walking down the hall toward us, when I noticed my dick was sticking out of my dickeys. Quickly I grabbed the coat and placed it on my lap.

He walked behind her and put his hands behind her hair. I tried not to look. I couldn't help thinking that she was a slut. She asked what took him so long. He cursed her, as if to impress me. He asked her to come to the bedroom for a sec. They went, and he slammed the door. Silence followed.

Minutes went by. Silence turned into moans and groans. My finger still had her juices on it. For a second I wanted to take his car, but I knew I wouldn't get far. Besides, whether he respected me or feared me, I didn't want to hurt him too bad. So I waited. Amanda got louder, as if she wanted to antagonize me.

He opened the door to the bedroom about twenty minutes later and headed back to the bathroom. I could still hear her breathing. I got off the couch and pretended to get a drink to replace the one she'd spilled earlier. On the way to the kitchen I put my head in the hallway and smiled at her. She looked like she had just gotten beaten up. Her skin was flushed and her lips were bigger, but she still was hot. Now I was ready. I headed to the living room and paced. Chris came out and said: "I'm ready. I just had to release some stress."

"I'm the one who should be releasing some fucking stress," I said, and I headed for where I left the coat.

Without saying a word, Chris and I walked out of the house and got in the car. He slowly pulled out the driveway, and asked me where I wanted to go. I told him to drive me back towards my house. As we passed a shopping outlet, I instructed him to pull inside. I reached down revealing the Uzi rolled up in the jacket. I put the leather strap over my shoulder just as before, Chris looked at me as if he wanted to ask me something, but said nothing. Though it was hot, I put the long black coat on. I shook Chris's hand and left him. He was relieved that he was not going to be a part of what I was about to do.

As Chris drove off, I thought of the wonderful home he would be returning to and it angered me. *If only I had what he had I wouldn't be in this mess*, I thought. This was my last thought as I walked through the parking lot looking for prospects.

"So what exactly were you looking for?" asked the Doctor.

"I wasn't sure exactly. Just someone who was alone, someone that looked like they wouldn't fight back, someone who was not aware of their surroundings, and someone who appeared to know nothing about people like me." Daniel said calmly. Then he continued.

I noticed a white man about my height, 5'7" heading towards his car. He was professionally dressed and had a look that said: "I'm not worried about nothing. Everything is great. I have money, a hot girl, and a few cars."

Some people will say: "When you work hard you can get these great material things." I never really enjoyed taking things from people who had worked hard for them. But this guy looked like he'd never worked a day in his life. So I decided this would be the longest day of his life.

I lit a Newport cigarette. I walked in his direction, then turned, as if I were headed towards a car near his. He saw me turning away from his path, and relaxed. As he unlocked his gold Infinity and got in, I suddenly veered toward him, asking: "Excuse me sir, can you give the directions to the nearest highway?"

He rolled the car window down. I repeated: "Can you tell me how to get to the nearest highway?"

The man put the key in the ignition and pointed straight with his index finger. "Go straight and make a right you'll run right in to it," he replied cheerfully.

I meant to tell him to get the fuck out of his car, but just then I felt escaping flatulence from last night's dinner. I'd missed my best opportunity. I changed tactics. "Sir, I have a very bad problem with directions. Can you please write it down."

The man looked at me in disgust and repeated the directions in a condescending tone.

This was the edge I needed. As he pretended to look for a pen, I opened my jacket and pointed the gun, still strapped to my shoulder, in the car window. "Get out the car," I ordered. He put his hands up and I opened the car door. "Give me your wallet."

He complied. To my amazement, he asked my permission to get his belongings from the back seat. His voice was calm and polite, so I let him do it. As I got into the driver seat I told him to hurry up. I thought he was stalling.

He said: "I have one more thing in the trunk."

I paused, then shouted: "No!" I shouted.

He closed the back car door. I put the car in reverse and smashed the gas. In my rearview mirror I saw him standing in the middle of the road, his face pained as he pleaded for people to call the cops. No one answered.

I had no idea how to get to where I was going, but I knew I had to get out of Dodge. I tried to find the highway but couldn't. I decided to just drive. I drove and drove until I saw my middle school. Pulling in the parking lot, I picked up the car phone and called my cousin Bryan for advice. I told him what was going on, I could tell he was excited; we talked about all the shit we were going to get into when I reached Ohio. About an hour passed. I told him I should get moving. He suggested that I just head north until I see a gas station, then run in and get a map. I headed north unaware of the speed signs or for that matter any signs.

I came to a bridge, but when I thought I was going underneath it, I found myself driving into opposing traffic. I'd entered the highway from the wrong side. Sitting on the off ramp, cars seemed to head right for me. I knew if one of those cars decided to get off, I would be dead. I had to get off that exit. As another car started to come past me I braced myself, jumped behind the car as it passed me, and made a U-turn onto the expressway. I hear another car. Tires screeched, rubber gripped the road, and tore.

I let go a sigh of relief as I gained speed. I cruised for an hour and a half, then looked for a gas station. I needed a map. I took the first exit, picked up the phone and called Bryan again. As I reached the gas station, I told him to stay on the phone and not to hang up.

Walking into the gas station, I started to feel that I'd gotten away with it. I looked through a stack of maps for the one that I thought I needed. I decided on the one that could get me the furthest.

I paid for my map and headed towards the car. Nothing moved, and there were no other cars. Even for a Sunday this was quiet. I glanced at my marble. It was black, I was overpowered with emotions. I felt anger and confusion. My heart raced, my stomach turned, and I knew something was very wrong. As I reached down to pick up the car phone, I heard what sounded like the screeching of wheels. Looking up I saw I was surrounded.

"Freeze! Don't fucking move, nigger! I'll blow your head off!"

I froze because he'd told me to.

The officer stuck the shotgun in my face. He threw me against the car, searched me, and told me how bad I stunk. He placed everything from my pockets, including my marble, in a zip lock bag. He and the other cops argued about what car to put me in. He pulled a gun out of the trunk of the car that I stole, but it wasn't my Uzi. The officer asked his partner if the victim had a permit for the weapon. He replied no, but to just let it go. Then I recalled the victim's eyes, and realized he'd been ready to shoot me. I'd had no intention of shooting him, but he wanted to kill me. I had escaped death once again.

I let my head fall back on the cop car seat. I tried to sleep. We drove for what seemed like hours. I closed my eyes, dreaming of the place that I would never find: Halisaseas. When the cop car stopped I opened my eyes and it was dark outside. I was exhausted. I noticed a small white building. It looked like a flimsy structure. Who could come here and help me escape, I wondered. The officers led me inside and handcuffed me to a bench.

They laughed and joked about what was going too happen to me in prison. I thought it was funny too. They didn't realize I wanted to be there. I laid my head back and listened as they talked like schoolgirls.

THIS PAGE LEFT INTENTIONALLY BLANK

CHAPTER 13

I fell asleep handcuffed to the bench. Two officers in brown uniforms woke me up. They were more relaxed than the officer who arrested me. They released me from the cuffs, and grabbed a handful of chains from behind the counter. They shackled my legs with these, connecting the chains to a thick brown leather belt they put around my waist. The belt also had handcuffs to restrain my wrists.

This didn't bother me. I had been tied up several times, always involuntarily. I was taken to a van and chained to the seat. We drove to a detention center. It wasn't one I knew. During my first couple of months there I heard nothing about my case. I later received court papers. At the top they said: "The state of ALABAMA vs. DANIEL BLACK." They listed two counts of first-degree armed robbery, and the charge of carjacking a public official. The maximum sentence for each count was 20 years. I didn't mind.

I waited for a court date but it didn't come. I got to know the staff. They even made me a trustee. I was okay. I could have whatever leftovers I wanted from dinner, and sometimes the staff would share snacks that they brought from home. Late at night I would fold the girls and boys clothes. I enjoyed it. I knew that was the closest I would ever get to another girl squash. The girls were separated from the boys.

The staff was great. We laughed when we saw the same kids come back in there, then leave, only to show up again for some other crime. Occasionally, I would get in trouble for not following orders. When this happened they put me in the hole where I could get a glimpse of the girls pod. Sometimes when I got into fights they would slam me on the floor, put my hands behind my back and make me grab my ears. Most of the time it took two people. It really hurt. Sometimes I would assist them when they were restraining other juveniles.

There were many fights. I settled my differences in the laundry room, or a staff member would open the prisoner's cell door for me by pushing a button. If a staffer had a headache, and just one person was causing all the problems, we would be put in lockdown for anywhere from 24 to 72 hours. Then I would lead the others in beating the shit out of the persistent troublemaker. The staff always knew about my hits. They understood that I kept order. Many people waiting there tried to escape, but the ones who tried were always brought back quickly.

I loved going to church in the detention center, because I always got to see some of the girls. I swore to myself that I would marry one someday. These girls would tell their stories, then I would carry my images of them back to my cell—quickly so as not to lose the fantasy.

I talked to one girl in particular during Bible study. Her name was Evan. She told me about all kinds of things she did for her boyfriend. I wished I were him, and free to break her out of jail. Evan's skin was a rich coca color; she was short, not thick, but not skinny. She was 4'7", weighed about 105, and was a C cup. I folded her underwear, so even before she approached me at my table, I knew the way her butt was shaped. Though she never suspected it, I fucked her every night.

Evan was soon released. After that I started getting bored. I felt as if the walls were closing in on me. Where was my marble? I wondered, and where was my friend? In nine months I didn't get a single visitor. I stopped caring. Holidays passed, friends came and went, and while no one messed with me, that just meant I had no one to beat up. When I was taken off of trustee duty I tried to kill myself several times. Once I tried it with a plastic spoon; and then I attempted to crack my head on the concrete slab.

The only time I could vividly remember was the moment when I sharpened the spoon and started hacking at my veins. It tired me out, and I sat, letting warm blood run down my arms. It felt like all the stress was draining out of me. This was interrupted by a loud noise. The next thing I knew, they were hooking me up to an IV bag. That time I never even left the detention center.

Once they put me in lockdown for 72 hours. I was naked, just like my friend from the woods had been when we first met.

I thought about standing on the metal sink and falling backwards again to crack my head, but I wasn't sure if that would work. Now I'm not even sure whether I did it. Finally my court date was approaching. The staffers said my suicide attempts might affect my hearing.

They wrapped my arms, and I was dressed in clothes that were acceptable to wear in a courtroom. They took me there by back roads. These led to the back entrance of the building. I wasn't scared. They could give me five years or sixty, and I would be ready.

First we met with the prosecutor. He told my public defender what I was charged with, and said I ought to take a plea bargain. I listened to what he said. He wasn't asking me to snitch on anyone. I took the deal. There was no trial. The public defender told the judge that by the time I got out of prison, it would be too late. My life would be set into that pattern. He argued that prison would corrupt me, making me a danger to their kids. He wanted the judge to keep me in the juvenile system until I was 18. Then I would get a second chance. I felt like killing him for saying something so stupid. *Why does he threaten the judge?* I thought to myself.

One of my fellow inmates had told me about his day in court before this same judge. When the judge sentenced him to two years for violating his probation, my friend responded: "I can do that standing on my head." The judge gave him six more years "to do on your feet." I wasn't scared, but I wasn't stupid.

Before I'd entered the courtroom a minister had been praying for me. From the sound of his prayer it seemed he wanted the judge to get confused and give me a second chance—as if my only hope was in misunderstandings. Before the judge passed down sentence he decided to recess court. When I turned around, there was my mother crying. I hadn't seen her in so long. In that absence, I had decided to let her go. I felt as if I barely knew this woman. She'd brought the minister of our church, but I didn't really know him either.

Finally the judge returned. He and the lawyers consulted in whispers. The judge finally spoke of my confused future, and ruled that he would give me a second chance. I wasn't sentenced to practically a lifetime behind bars, but I would have to remain locked up for awhile. I stood up and thanked the court. As I was on my way out, my mother asked to hug me. My keepers wouldn't let her, and I didn't even look at her. In the next couple of days they began processing me so I could leave the detention center. It took longer to get out than to get in. Finally my papers were complete, and it was my turn to be discharged.

I thought that wherever they were taking me was bound to have more freedom then the detention center. I gathered my belongings. They took me to the loading dock where again I was shackled from head to toe. I asked my guards if they'd gotten my belongings from the property room. They said they had, but I had to sign to get them back. I did. That's when I saw my marble again, but I could not keep it. They were giving it to the transporter.

CHAPTER 14

We took a long drive to a place in Alabama called Roebuck. It was a facility about the size of a community college. As we approached the campus, one of the guards told us stories of people trying to escape. Some got killed in the process. I knew this was just to scare us. I was just happy to be away from my mom and her family.

As we waited to be processed they took off the chains and ordered us to disrobe. One-by-one we were told to squat and cough—a humiliating experience. I thought one of the guys was homosexual. I had nothing against his sexual preference, but I didn't much like it in a place like this. I felt that it wasn't fair. Why couldn't I be locked up with people I was attracted to? His sexual behavior was his business, but I knew that, if he looked at me again, I was going to fuck him up.

The staff inventoried our belongings. Over the past year in lockup, I had acquired some necklaces and valuables, and they listed these. We were then led to 9' by 12' cells. Aside from bunks, the only things in each cell were a Bible and a metal toilet. *This could be home*, I said to myself.

We sat in our cells, wearing only the underwear they'd given to us when we arrived. Though some boys would flood their cells, all that got them was oily water they had to sit in. The water was so cold your feet would easily get numb. Some guys cried. Others talked about how they were going to rape the ones who were crying. I did pushups. I chuckled as I watched the other new inmates lose what sanity they had. It was better than HBO.

On the third morning, a young light-skinned boy peeked into my cell, and handed me a sheet under the door. I placed my foot on the door and pulled hard. A blanket came next, then a low-rider magazine with nude pictures folded up inside it. I knew I would have to pay for his generosity.

The next night we were sent to a minimum security building on the other side of the facility. It was a little warmer than the maximum security holding cells. They told me that if I caused problems I would go back. I assumed we'd spent three days in maximum security so we'd be familiar with the punishments for disobeying. Little did they know, I'd grown up in those types of cells.

In the next year I heard everybody's story of why they were incarcerated. Every day it was the same routine: wake up at 0600 hours, clean up and shower, then breakfast, school, lunch, and counseling. Afterwards we went to our cells until dinner. After dinner we would get a couple hours of recreation; cards, ping-pong, and shit-talking. The weekend was different. If we behaved we were allowed to watch movies or go outside. We were always supervised.

I got good grades in their unstructured educational program. It was more like being home-schooled. I went to anger counseling and Alcoholics Anonymous twice a week. One of the guards was a Muslim. I told him I had taken the Oath and I was ready to lead people to Allah. I knew it was wrong. He assisted me in anything I needed. Our congregation was not going to eat anything out of the cafeteria from then on. It was hard. I had nothing better to do with my time, but complain and go on strike. This worked.

We got our own food and our own cooks. That alone brought people to hear what I had to say. I knew these inmates wanted an easy way out. They wanted to feel different—special. I was able to provide them with that.

Our congregation sat together during breakfast lunch and dinner. We used that time to talk about defending ourselves. We also talked about what we needed like, clothes, food, books, smokes, and drinks—everything but sex—and tried to find ways to get them. Sometimes I could get contraband for people. The guards soon caught on to our organized crime and transferred me to a maximum security building.

During visitation, I learned that the guy who had given me the contraband was my Uncle Bill's stepson or some such relation. We became friends, but I did not trust him. He was envious of my power to persuade people. I hated the new unit I was in. It was always cold. The tables were bolted to the floor and we received very little recreational time. The rooms were always locked and we had to communicate through the air vents. Even the showers were horrible. I had no privacy. Others could look through the little rectangular Plexiglas window on the shower door and watch me.

A new guard had arrived, a Black Panther. He was a skinny old guy and wore a leather jacket all the time. He admired me and gave me a bracelet made of red, black and green fabric, almost like the primary colors of my marble. I longed for that marble; it was my symbol of power. We talked about how the government wasn't designed to rehabilitate you. You must rehabilitate yourself. He pointed out that the government wanted to return all the young black inmates who got released to prison. He said that when these young men were released, they weren't mentally prepared for society. He said young men like me would return to the only way of life we knew. Then the authorities would point the finger and say: "We knew he would end up in prison." He argued that racism still existed, but it had been modernized. We always argued because I didn't always see things his way but I respected him. I respected everybody even my white racist friends who hated every black but me.

The black panther guy didn't make me seek his approval for anything. He put me on trustee duty, which allowed me to be out of my cell all the time. I got whatever food, and all the blankets I wanted. When I would slap someone, he would usually turn his head, figuring they might deserve it.

On the other hand Uncle Bill's relative was a loudmouthed troublemaker. He'd lived in Alabama long enough to make a few friends, and he'd joined the gang known as the Crips. I couldn't be a part of what he was doing; he had too much attention on him. Eventually he got jealous of me.

One Saturday afternoon we were headed out to the rec yard, when I soon heard a loud shout. A fight broke out. This was nothing new to me, so I squatted and watched. On the back of my head I felt something like a bee sting. It was him.

"What the fuck are you doing?" I demanded.

He kept on coming, punching everywhere like a confused child. I could see that he didn't have control of himself, but by the time I decided to kick his ass we were all on the ground. I looked at him, wondering what made him so angry, Ultimately, it didn't matter. I knew I had to get back at him. My reputation kept me safe, and if I let him get away with that, I'd have never-ending problems.

After the disturbance, everybody was on lockdown. My Black Panther friend came to my cell. I told him what happened, and that Uncle Bill's relative had to pay. He said I should be smart about it. The next day they released everyone from their cells. Uncle Bill's relative refused to come out. I knew this meant he was preparing himself. That wasn't good.

The next day I sharpened a toothbrush on my concrete bed. When the cells opened for breakfast, I took off towards his. He had no time to get ready. I beat the shit out of him.

The guard pulled me by the pants. "Come on, Daniel." What he meant was: hurry up. The relative's homemade shank went flying down the stairs. I stabbed him in the side with my toothbrush, and he slipped down the stairs.

When they brought the incident before a board, the charge against me was dropped. They agreed that it had been self-defense. Finally the system worked for me. I didn't get off completely though. I got a week in the hole for the shank, and they moved me to another maximum security building. One staff member there was always reading books on philosophy and history. He explained to me that colors had powers, and that the entire universe was connected by mathematical principles. He told me to focus on the numbers 3, 5, and 7. He wore what seemed to be a fraternity ring, and he told me that he was a Shriner. I told him I wanted to be one.

"Not yet," he said with a humble smile. "You're not old enough."

He started giving me book after book to read. He was in politics, and seemed to have a characteristic prestige. I was sure he was going to be the next president. But then I figured that the thought of having a black president was preposterous.

About two-and-a-half years passed. My life was becoming boring. My gym coach was a Mason. He talked to me every day, and taught me a lot about life. I had good friends, but now it was time for me to move on. I had learned a lot, I had fought a lot.

The people in charge said I was getting to old for their facility, so I was out-processed to go to Mount Meigs. That's when I found out all of my belongings had been stolen, even my marble. I didn't have much, but cherished what I did have, so this bothered me. Other inmates told me that the gay guy who came in with us, Fred, had stolen a lot of things from the property room. I thought there was nothing I could do about it.

THIS PAGE LEFT INTENTIONALLY BLANK

CHAPTER 15

The campus at Mt. Meigs, Alabama wasn't much different from Roebuck, except that it was about the size of a university campus, and we could see the state pen's watchtower. The guys there were older. Most were in for serious crimes. After my intake I was put in a tank for 72 hours, the same as before. I had at least three years left, so I was considered a serious juvenile offender. They put me in a unit that was a lot like a dorm. It wasn't as strict as the other facilities. The building was the size of two double-wide trailers put together. The walls and floors were easily penetrable, so you could get in and out of rooms easily. There were no locks in this building, not even on the front door. I immediately paid an inmate for a razor blade and put it in my mouth for my safety. I kept it there for the next six months.

One guy had been in there since he was 9. When I arrived he was 17. He was a very tall slinky white boy who didn't talk much. I came to find out that he had killed his mom and a store clerk. He'd then put them in a trunk, and gone to a skating ring. He had a laptop, a desktop, a recliner and a TV.

He was very smart. While there he'd earned his G.E.D, so he could now take college classes. He could get permission for unsupervised trips outside the facility. The guy's family still came to visit him. When his grandparents came they always brought food for the staff.

It was great there; we had a female staffer with short hair, red bone and a perfect body. Though the male staffers hated it, all the guys hit on her. Sometimes they put her on the spot, telling her about crushes. The staff didn't understand what was happening. In their ignorance, they were allowing the inmates the opportunity to disrespect her. Guys started showing her their privates as they exited the showers. That got them in trouble.

She was really nice and studied a lot, so I asked her to help me prepare for my G.E.D. We got to be real close. Sometimes I was out of my cell all night. Another inmate started getting jealous, and thought he could punk me. I quickly slapped the shit out of him. All they did was send me to my room for the day; no big deal. The staffer adored me. We became friends. The male guards had no choice but to respect me, but sometimes they would fuck with me to make her mad.

One night while she was doing laundry, I came in and saw her bending over, and pulling clothes out the washer. I couldn't help myself. I put my hands on her back, as if to help her. She didn't move. This would've been enough to put me in prison, but the staffer turned around, grabbed my arm, and smiled. She slid her hands down my arm, gently stopping me. I immediately went back to my room and jacked off. I wanted her to catch me, but I think she knew what I was doing, and never came. About two minutes later, I came out. I sat down and watched TV while the clothes finished. She looked at me, shook her head and smiled. No shame in my game. She didn't help me with the clothes anymore that night.

Sometime later a guy got caught letting Fred, the gay guy, suck his dick. Fred was then sent to my building. I felt he owed me for my jewelry and marble, so I beat him up several times. Finally there came a day when I found my marble and watch on my bunk. But I continued to beat him. He hadn't returned all my stuff, and besides, it was like he enjoyed it. As I slapped him around he kept saying "yes sir" and "no sir." He was too nice and polite to beat up, so instead I extorted him. I made him sell Newports for me at a dollar a square. Every Wednesday I would receive his commissary, two honey buns and one Snickers. It was a good life. But then he started giving another guy his commissary. It was a guy I'd slapped when I first came to Mount Meigs. Fred and his new boyfriend paid a severe price. I cracked his boyfriend in the head with a lock-in-a-sock. Just as I did it, other inmates rushed into Fred's room, dragged them both out, and started beating them. This turned into a minor riot.

This put us all on lockdown. We couldn't go outside, and had to eat in our rooms for three days. That was okay. I was still a trustee, so the rules didn't apply to me. People bonded with me. Fred had caused these problems often, and everyone was waiting for the right moment to get him. It was just a matter of time.

One night, when the female staffer was working, I found her again in the laundry room. I came up behind her and grabbed her ass. Suddenly I felt like I'd ejaculated into my pants, and my drawers felt a little sticky. She turned around and said: "No!" It was if I were a puppy that had done something wrong.

"I'm sorry," I said.

"That's okay," she said. "Now finish these clothes." She walked away.

Though I felt remorse, I also thought it was partly her fault.

Eight months later a guy raped her in the utility closet with a broomstick. They sent the guy to prison, she resigned. That left me feeling lonely. I failed my G.E.D. Then, while we were on lockdown, I went to the kitchen to get our food. There I met a woman who worked in the kitchen. She had a daughter who was also around. The daughter and I fell in love. Often she gave me hand jobs. One day I told the staff that her mom wanted me to help in the kitchen. They believed me so I started spending much more time there.

One day in the back the daughter and I were washing dishes. When her T-Shirt got wet, I couldn't help but notice her nipples. I looked and smiled. She took my hand and put it on her breast. I nodded towards the storage closet. I told her to take off her underwear. She was scared so I slid my hands down, feeling her slick sweaty public hairs; she was wet. It tasted bitter sweet. She grabbed my cock. As she kissed me her breath stunk but I didn't care. She jerked hard on my cock, but then we heard her mom calling her. That time I didn't cum.

I wanted that girl so bad. We finished the dishes and I returned to my unit. After that they never tried to put inmates in the kitchen again, and the civilian contractors were no longer allowed to have inmates help them. I decided to try and take my G.E.D again. I'd participated in a program to scare young kids so they wouldn't wind up in the correctional system. I even wrote a report on my idea of what a criminal was. I said that most people were criminal in some ways. Some cheat on taxes, some jaywalk, and just about everybody drives too fast. In my report I wrote that these kinds of acts often led to greater crimes. The problem wouldn't emerge until their crimes turned serious, threatening the money or safety of others. Those little crimes were like gateway drugs. Little crimes were a lot like alcohol. Most people did those things, but the ones who lived in families or surroundings where crime was everywhere, were more susceptible to becoming dangerous.

We all had to see therapist. Mine was ugly and about 50 years old. I still tried to fantasize about her but it didn't work.

One day, while I was studying for my G.E.D an 11-year-old boy came in and sat at the table. All the nearby teenagers were picking with him. I told them to back off. I asked the boy: "What did you do to wind up here?"

"I killed my brother."

"Oh, shit," I said, smiling.

The nearby inmates started chanting about C-murder, a famous rapper. That's the name they were calling this kid.

I told them: "You guys better stop fucking with people."

He didn't look like a killer. He had glasses and looked like a nerd.

"What happened?" I asked.

"I didn't mean to kill him," he said. "I only hit him in the head once with a bat." But he'd also hidden the body in the freezer. It was all over a pizza.

C-murder went to school with us and got picked on every day. I wanted to help but I was tired of fighting. He had to walk his own path.

Every day at school the older guys would beat the shit out of younger ones. I asked the staff to segregate the schools by age, but they did not listen. There was nothing I could do. Another Black Panther guard had my back. Because I practiced the Muslim faith, he thought I was associated with the Nation of Islam. I wasn't I like everyone and every race.

The Black Panther tried to convince me that white people were devils. He said a scientist had been experimenting, and when the experiment went bad, that cast the Caucasian race onto some mountain or something. I thought he was crazy and didn't believe a word he said.

My best friend was the son of a Russian mobster.

"Why doesn't your dad get you out?" I asked.

"Because I caused him too many problems, and drew too much attention," he said.

Just like I did with my father, I thought.

My other friend was from the gang MS 3. He was insane, and would fight anywhere anytime. One day they locked him in the hole and he flooded the tank and smeared shit over the window. Both of my friends protected me, though I never knew why. I didn't have any reason not to like white people. Most of them were smarter than the black people I was locked up with.

The Doctor said that I was experiencing a lot. "Did you think anything they were telling you was true?" he asked.

"Well, Doc," Daniel responded, "my mom always told me to take in the good and throw out the bad."

White people were the ones that kept me out of trouble. It was mostly black people who tried to get me into fights. I started to turn more to the Bible but it was hard. I was confused and was not living right. I prayed for wisdom, knowledge and understanding. One night I woke up to my marble spinning on the side of my mat. It was turning purple. I sat up and folded my legs Indian-style, and placed the marble between my hands as it continued to spin. I remember humming and going into a mysterious chant. I thought about the guy in the woods, and then my so-called family, who had all abandoned me. I didn't even know the name of the guy in the woods.

I remember seeing myself from the corner of the cell. I was looking down at myself sitting there. I tried to get the attention of this boy-who-was-me, but he didn't move. I thought: *I am dreaming.* I didn't feel like myself. I tried to ask myself questions: What's my name? Who am I?

The name Aadil came up. I hadn't heard that in a long time. I realized that, if this wasn't a dream, I could go anywhere I pleased. I thought of where I wanted to go and just like that I was there. I could see everybody, and nobody could see me, but I could feel it was real, even my mother's prayers. Then I heard a loud click. I was being pulled back to the jail. When I opened my eyes, they were dry. A staffer was beating a trashcan for head call.

It was six o'clock in the morning. I hid my marble in my mattress. I never knew what I'd experienced that day, but I thanked God for answering my prayers. It might explain my sharpened intuition. From then on I knew how to recognize certain signs and avoid problems. I also knew how to do many things that I still can't explain. I became a great problem solver. I read the entire Bible, the Quran, and many other books. My deferential perception would become a complicated obstacle.

"Ask, and it shall be given you; seek, and ye shall find; knock, and it shall be opened unto you." Matthew 7:7

Many of Islam's teachings are similar to those in the Bible. I decided it was good to pray to God five times a day, and to fast for thirty days a year; it felt right. The only thing I was stuck on was Islam's teaching that Jesus is a prophet. However, the Quran also said that Christians will go to heaven and the Sabians will have their reward.

Then I looked at the Bible again. It said that if you don't believe that Jesus died for your sins, you will not go to heaven. I took this to mean that if I were a Christian and lived as Jesus did, I would go to heaven. Christianity also teaches that if you truly ask for forgiveness in the name of Jesus, you will be forgiven. We are born in a state of sin, hence we must be baptized.

Islam teaches that your sins will be weighed, and you will pay for your mistakes; I had made a lot of mistakes. That made it obvious: I couldn't go wrong if I turned to Jesus. However, I felt I was not ready. I didn't realize that you could come to him in any state. I'd read in the Quran that you cannot approach God (Allah) when you are unclean, mentally or physically. According to the Quran, if you did this, the angels would not hear you.

"Surely, those who appreciate, and those who are Jewish, and the Sabians, and the Christians--whoever appreciates God and the Last Day and does good, will have nothing to fear nor will they grieve." *Quran 5:69*

"For God so loved the world that he gave his one and only begotten Son, that whoever believes in him shall not perish but have eternal life." John 3:16

"When Jesus spoke again to the people, he said, 'I am the light of the world. Whoever follows me will never walk in darkness, but will have the light of life.'" John 8:12

I finally concluded that the devil would come in disguise—perhaps a snake—and he would try to twist the word of God to suit his own purposes. I knew that the best lies contain a little bit of truth. The devil's main weapon is confusion. He wants us to fight over religons. God does not need us to fight. We need him.

So the truth was clear but I was not ready. I was confused, and searching for inner peace, but I didn't know how to get it. There was so much deception in the world that the truth would be almost impossible to find. Why should I seek it if the world didn't want me to know about it?

Wanting to know everything, I studied many religions, even Buddhism. Time after time I would go to church, spiritually falling down, and getting back up. People would say: "He is a Muslim," and the minister would say, "He is going to hell, but he can stay." This discouraged me, but I kept going back.

The minister didn't like me, and couldn't answer my questions, but in the end this didn't bother me. I kept going there just to listen and eat. In my cell I prayed to God in the name of Jesus: "If I am meant to be released then let it be, but until then show me the light." Soon I didn't feel alone in my cell, and the devil got off my back. Every night I prayed for my sins to be forgiven. I wanted people to stop returning. Soon humility began to grow in me. I didn't worry about being incarcerated or getting out. I only worried about improving myself as a man. I felt free.

C-murder was caught up in the gangs and owed people money. For his own safety they moved him to another maximum security building. I was in my fifth year of incarceration when I finally passed my G.E.D. I went to the school to help the teachers, and studied in my room.

A 9-year-old white boy came in for molesting and suffocating his baby sister. Fred and a few guys started to pick on this boy. I wondered why these sexual offenders messed with each other. Hadn't they been picked on enough? This boy was just a child. I could only protect him at school.

One day Fred and his friends raped the boy, nearly beating him to death. He wound up in the hospital, and never returned to Mount Meigs. An investigation took place. I'd told them they should put him in protection, but nobody listened. I'd hoped my newfound higher power would allow me to leave it in God's hand, but that didn't work.

"Why couldn't you?" The Doctor asked.

"Because there was so much more I needed to learn in life. I needed to see for myself. It's like when the government gives people the death penalty, and the victim's family watches. I felt if I did not do anything, they would get away with it, and hurt somebody else." Daniel responded.

So I had to take matters in my own hands. I wanted Fred and his friends to feel some suffering. I gathered my friends and school customers who I'd supplied with free cigarettes. I was determined to send the molesters to the hospital.

Walking in the hallway I saw my victims. They never knew what was coming. With one leg sweep one boy went down. After I stomped his head on the wax floor, my boys dragged the other two guys into a classroom. God knows what they did to them. I walked away. Afterwards the entire campus was on lockdown for a week.

After that I left my Muslim heritage behind completely, and went to church constantly. I asked for forgiveness. I prayed to God for wisdom, knowledge and understanding. I went up before the warden, a retired army officer. I told him I wanted to join the army. He told me if I did he would release me early, around my eighteenth birthday. I told him I would enlist, so he asked me to come back a month later for an evaluation. I was good and stayed to myself. I lived in a minimum security facility now. One evening I returned to my room to find a hole in the wall. All my cigarette-sale money was gone. I learned that Bill's stepson, the one from Roebuck, had come to Mount Meigs. Fred had my money.

I was still fighting my dark side, but I put an order out this time to hurt them both. Over the next week, anybody who'd been involved in the theft got stabbed or beaten up.

The warden called me in. "Daniel, do you want to go home?" he asked.

"Yes, sir," I said.

"Then it stops, now!" he insisted.

I paused. I wanted to say, "What, sir?" I resisted doing that, and instead I shook my head, indicating I would do as he said. That was it. Two weeks later I was packing my belongings.

The Doctor looked at Daniel.

Daniel handed him the marble. "You know, Doc, I can't take this place anymore."

The Doctor replied: "Daniel do you want to continue to be in the military?"

"No doc" Daniel responded, "I want to be free."

"Ok then please don't hurt anybody."

Daniel returned to his routine, but felt as if he were seconds away from losing his mind. He made it until Friday. Would the Doctor have good news for him? Daniel was disappointed that all the Doc wanted was for him to finish the story.

THIS PAGE LEFT INTENTIONALLY BLANK

CHAPTER 16

My next stop was a group home—more like a halfway house—in Mobile,

Alabama. We drove up to a house that was large, but not so big as to attract

attention. It sat on the corner of the road, facing the hospital where I'd

been born. Some shade trees concealed its real purpose from the neighbors.

When we pulled into the front driveway, the place reminded me of a

retirement home.

Dragging my chains, I walked up the handicap ramp. I went inside,

knowing I was somewhat of a spectacle. In jail I had learned to be free in

my mind by accepting the things I could not change, but if I was truly free,

why was I still in chains?

The staff at the group home asked that my chains be removed. With

every clink I felt more relieved. They led me to the left, through what

appeared to be a huge living room. A boy of about 16 sat at the table eating

soup. He looked depressed. I thought: *He must not have gotten a visit today*. A white woman who looked like a bodybuilder gave me a brown bag, and told me to proceed to the recreation room.

The brown bag contained a baloney sandwich, a bag of chips, and an apple. Now I knew why the guy was eating soup. The juveniles came running in, as if they'd known I was there. I already knew some of them because they'd spent time in other facilities with me. One of them asked: "Hey did you find out who took your money?"

"Yes, I did," I replied.

He looked at me. "What are you going to do about it?'

"Nothing," I said, as if the thought appalled me.

They knew my cousin hadn't been punished for the theft. Within a few days they were picking on me. I saw them as animals. They thought I was weak, because I'd agreed to join the army. I didn't care. It was over for me. I wanted a new life.

My first week there I had no privileges, and couldn't go anywhere. This meant early bedtime and no weekend liberty. I didn't say much to anybody. Even though I had my G.E.D, they still required me to participate in home school. They picked on me constantly, but, when someone slapped me, I walked away.

Most of the boys were there from two weeks to a few months. They seemed to have a pretty good life. Most had people who loved them. We went to the skating rink, and their parents came every weekend. Many of them had girlfriends. One or two had messed up families, maybe even worse then mine. Those were the ones who were glad to be locked up, but they also got picked on.

I had never skated in my life. I didn't do well at the skating rink, or with the girls. We all had chores, and we were allowed to have money, but I was tired of going out on the weekends. I knew nothing about girls. Most girls were afraid of me. Many of them didn't like dark-skinned boys.

I got paid to do chores while the other boys went out, and soon I bought a pair of blue and white Jordans. I wanted to fit in. I learned how to cut hair and made even more money. A month-and-a-half passed and I had to remind some people who I was. I had three months until my eighteenth birthday. A guy didn't want to pay me for a haircut so I slapped him a couple of times. I was upset because people were taking advantage of me. He had the money, but he'd decided to spend it elsewhere. He took my kindness for weakness, so I had to show him how it was. It was a close call. He reported me, but had no witnesses. All they did was take my weekend pass.

A new staffer, an old, wise black guy arrived. Besides giving orders, he didn't talk much. When we were lifting weights I noticed a Masonic sign around his neck. I told him I wanted to become one. He said: "Ask one to become one, seek and ye shall find." I stood there puzzled as he walked away.

An army recruiter came, and took me to be processed into the Army National Guard. They sent my mom a waiver she had to sign. I hadn't talked to her in some time. When she heard of my scheduled release she called, saying she was happy, but she thought I should have gone active duty.

She said my dad's best friend, Cedrick, would pick me up the following week. My dad was in prison. I agreed to this. Until my release, all I had to do was to keep to myself and stay out of trouble. To prepare for the army, I ran laps around the yard, and hid in the backyard lifting weights. The new staffer would check on me. One evening, he started talking about "the third eye." He said it was good for me to seek knowledge and wisdom. According to him the third eye was a kind of sensory perception that allowed its user to see into the depths of the world. He said that there is another world beyond this one. He was describing an out-of-body experience. It wasn't as mystical as it sounds. It was simply a way to see past all the treachery in the world.

He told me about the government and its conspiracies to control the world by laws and regulations. This included religious beliefs, beginning with the Catholics. The government intent was to confuse us, blinding us with their power, and with all material things. They conditioned us to kill each other to keep down the population. It was their way of managing resources. He said a few powerful men controlled governments, starting wars to balance good and evil, and maneuvering people in and out of high offices. He described the world as a bubble. He said I could use the third eye to insure that I would never again be locked up. He didn't think this world would last much longer. The only people who would survive were those with the knowledge. He believed that the prophecies in "Revelations" would occur. Though no one knew when, the world would indeed be destroyed.

I thought to myself that civilization might not want to know if certain things were true. For example, we might not want to know about aliens or secret experiments. It might be too much for common people to handle, so maybe it was best to be blind. I don't know what the world would be like without religion. It's the only think most people have. Then I thought of my primary marble hidden in my room. Whenever I had it I looked at the world from a different angle. I began to question religion. What if monotheistic religions were ways God talked to man. Each religion used a different angle because men were blind or thought differently. I wanted to know more, but apparently I was not ready.

Cedrick, my father's friend and my mother's ex-husband, came to pick me up. The discharge papers were signed. I was completely free.

"When's my dad getting out?" I asked him.

"A long time from now," he said.

Instead of going straight to South Carolina, they sent me to Georgia. I would be there until it was time for basic training. The bus ride was horrible. I was nervous, and watched everybody and everything, including my marble.

My mother and I decided to drive to South Carolina to see my sister Ashley. I would be there until it was time to go to boot camp. Adrian had gone into Job Corps. I had missed so much in life.

CHAPTER 17

They sent me to boot camp in Fort Benning, Goergia. During intake I had to put all my belongings in a brown paper bag. Once again I was forced to proceed without my marble. I was in basic training for infantry, the hardest basic training in the Army. I was up for the challenge.

We spent the first two days being processed, then the fun began. There were 60 other guys. I didn't talk them. Our Drill Sergeant told us to look to right then left. He said one of us would not be there by graduation. We learned about military history and tactics. The drill sergeants worked us about eighteen hours a day. They spit in our faces and pushed us to the limit. When one person messed up everybody paid for it. We had to work out, recite our military history and our chain of command before we could eat. Many people were not accustomed to the hazing, but I was. I talked to the others when they cried at night. When instructors screamed in my face, I wasn't fazed. In jail I'd learned how to mentally take myself out a place I didn't want to be.

When we ate we only had about two minutes. Some people snuck food back to the barracks. We all had to pay for any contraband found during inspections. This included food and inappropriate pictures, and resulted in about three hours of repetitive exercise. The exercise made people throw up.

The Doctor asked, "So, is this when you were in the Army?"

"Yes," Daniel said.

The Doctor wasn't really paying attention anymore. Daniel knew this because the Doctor stopped taking notes.

The ones who caused problems were disciplined at night. They were beaten with a sock holding a bar of military-issue soap, small and square, like hotel soap, but 2 inches thick. The sounds from those being disciplined were horrifying. A couple of dozen privates were venting their frustrations on these troublemakers.

We had locks on our wall lockers, and I was pleased no one thought of using them as weapons. Can you imagine how a sock with a lock in it, would crush the skull? The boys traded pictures of their sisters and ex-girlfriends for other things, like boot polish or stamps, just like in jail. Over half the privates lost their girlfriends or wives during training. Some nights morale dissolved, and all we had were the cadences that we sang all day to motivate us.

One Private would call out: "O Lord, I want to go." Another would sing: "...home..." and we all would join in. The drill sergeants would come out screaming and yelling, but I knew they were pleased. We were motivating each other.

Due to my size and antisocial characteristics, they promoted me to platoon guide. The drill sergeants did not want leaders who talked too much or needed friends. Some people would categorize some of my traits as narcissistic, antisocial, or even sociopathic.

The physical training was hard but all you had to do was obey orders. That was easy for me to do. We learned about explosives, navigating in the woods, and surviving off of nothing but nature. Weapons were my specialty. I could disassemble and reassemble my M-16 with my eyes closed, hanging upside down, in thirty seconds or less. We would run so much that by graduation two miles seemed like a walk in the park.

During the last two weeks the hardcore drill sergeants became our friends, and we begged for physical training. "More PT, Drill Sergeant!

More PT!" we would shout. We ran, breathing in the nose and out the mouth, till our legs collapsed. The best way to get promoted was to be fit so I did that. Near the end of training they woke us at 0300hrs. The drill sergeants told to prepare for a three-day field exercise. As I prepared the platoon I felt excited. Then the drill sergeant told me I was fired and to pick another platoon leader. I was learning to adapt, overcome, and practice the values of selflessness; naturally I promoted my best squad leader. I didn't know why I was fired. I also knew that, as leader, he would surely be promoted during graduation.

I didn't care; I just wanted to get moving. So we huddled around the new platoon leader waiting for orders. He was nervous and nobody respected him, so I had to lead from behind, serving others. As I gave them instructions he was quiet. After I lined them up outside in a staggered formation, I patted him on the back, signaling him to take charge. We headed out on a 45-mile hike, 15 miles a day, digging in every two or three miles.

On the third night it was snowing. We dug six-foot graves for our .50 caliber machine guns, and shallow graves for the solders with M-16s. It was the coldest I had ever been. We'd spent the previous two previous nights taking smoke grenades. We'd had to take cover from bombs that illuminated the sky. After three days we were exhausted.

The trees seemed to move by themselves. I felt safe, as if I had my marble. It felt like I was in a bubble impervious to all danger. We focused hard on our line of fire, swearing we saw people. Sometimes we would just open fire. When one solder shot, we all shot. The D.S would come by, kick you in your head, and throw a smoke bomb in your hole if you were sleeping. You had a battle buddy in the hole with you, and you only had one of everything. I remembered my battle buddy having to pee badly. He was crying because he couldn't feel his fingers. He said he could not get out of the sleeping bag or hole because he was too cold. I looked at the pain on his face and sarcastically told him to piss himself. He did, right there in the sleeping bag with the both of us in it. We both laughed and were warm for just a couple of minutes; this was the most humility I had ever showed.

The next morning I was put on mess duty and it was fun. I was able to eat as much as I wanted; the sergeants had explained that we all had a role in the mission. So I didn't mind feeding my platoon (which I knew was mine). Everyone else was complaining.

On the fourth day we returned to base and had a well-deserved warrior chow for lunch. I was made platoon leader again. When I marched out of the chow hall, my drill sergeant told me to get the platoon quiet. Everybody who was graduating knew it by then, so it was hard to keep them under control. I would drop them into pushup position and they would do the pushups with ease. I would get down with them to lead by example, but we didn't have time for working out. We had to prepare for graduation.

The drill sergeant was pissed, but that didn't bother anybody. They laughed and joked, and begged for more exercise. The drill sergeant told the platoon to gather around him and took off his belt and top. "Come on your motherfuckers" he said. Nobody came out so he started calling out my squad leaders. One-after-another he put them on the ground. I got excited as he got to my name.

"Private Black!"

"Yes, Drill SERGEANT!"

"Fighting position!"

In two minutes I took him to the ground and put him in the arm bar. I knew all I had to do was lift my waist and he would tap out, but I just held him. I kept him there long enough to let him know, if I wanted to, I could break his arm. Then I got a weird feeling, like sympathy. I loosened my grip on his wrist. He flipped over putting me in a rear naked choke. He was done and so was I. It was quiet as he ordered me to get the platoon in formation.

Graduation came and nobody was there to see me—same as when I was in jail. Nine weeks of hell. I'd done it with ease, but I hadn't gotten a promotion, though my squad leaders had. I thought I was left out because I could only get promoted so high during training. I was already an E-2 so I let it go. I didn't need anybody now. People had wives and mothers and sisters that showed up, but not me. That was okay. One other graduate was alone. His wife had run off with his recruiter, sending him a "Dear John" letter. I was there, and consoled him when he opened the letter. After graduation we hung out together. I looked forward to being reunited with my marble.

THIS PAGE LEFT INTENTIONALLY BLANK

CHAPTER 18

I went to Ohio for and stayed with my cousin Bryan before Advanced Individual Training (AIT). He lived with his mom on Avondale Street in Columbus. Most things had not changed; in fact they had gotten worse. At first his mom seemed okay, but I could tell she was being deceitful. My marble stayed yellow. She was overweight and sad inside. All day she did nothing but bark orders at him. He would clean from sunup to sundown.

I soon found out that Bryan had two kids. He asked me to watch his daughter while he cheated on his girlfriend. Meanwhile his mom would be in her room with "company". I remembered smelling an atrocious odor, like rotten eggs and spoiled fish, coming from her room. When Bryan returned home and asked where his mom was, I said she was in her room. As he walked in, she yelled at him: "Close the damn door!" I could see her stretched out on the bed with a sheet that barely covered her. It was like something on the Discovery Channel.

Bryan slept in the basement. He said all his mom did was turn tricks, I was appalled. I started folding the clothes for him as he cried. He never cleaned, and had me do his chores when I was there. He lay on the couch and talked about a girl he'd slept with named Angie, Sydney's girlfriend. He told me that she was coming over that night. She never showed up, so he called his girlfriend over. While they went out, I kept her friend company.

This friend was a minister's daughter. I didn't know anything about relationships, but I wanted one. I treated her with the utmost respect. She would pull on my clothes and reach for my penis, but for some reason I resisted. I tried to go out on a proper date with her the next night, but she said she was sick. I walked five miles and gave her flowers and candy. Her parents were pleased. I couldn't see her, but I asked them to deliver the get-well message. She later called me and said she didn't want to speak to me again. I was too nice, she said. I cried on the phone then cursed her out. She laughed and said good-bye. I told Bryan. He said he already slept with her anyway.

He always tried to get me laid with the girls he'd been with. I guess it was a way for him to move on to something new. His mom's friend, Angie, did come over eventually. I remembered her from our childhood. When she was taking a shower he told me to just walk in the bathroom and start eating her out.

I couldn't do it; the thought of oral sex at that point was repulsive. When his mother's birthday came around, I gave him a hundred dollars to give to her something, because I wanted her to feel better about her son. But he had more secrets, and soon I would find out what they were. He took me to see our cousin, Luke, who was gay and had a boyfriend named James. James was a white older guy who called himself a drag queen. However, the guy was intelligent and had money.

Bryan and Luke would take Luke's boyfriends on expeditions through the city, picking up guys and girls. I rode in back, puzzled, as we pulled up to a club downtown. My two cousins explained to me that I was too slow for Ohio. They said sometimes I had to front to get what I wanted. I ignored them. I knew I could rip their throats out if I wanted to, but they were family, so I let them be. Entering the club I noticed that it was all males and maybe a few females—not the kind of club I had hoped for. I was too respectful to say anything. They told me: "Fags always have money and most of them do cocaine." So this would be very lucrative for them. I didn't believe anything they said, but I wanted a drink, so I went along. A black guy named Poncho who was dressed like a cowboy approached me. He shook my hand in an unmanly way, then kissed me on the cheek. When I cursed him out, they kicked me out of the club. I punched the bouncer in the mouth.

When I got to Bryan's house, my two cousins left me. Soon after that there was a knock at the door. I opened it and it was Poncho. He apologized for what had happened, and said that my cousins had put him up to it, though he was attracted to me. He'd given my cousins Rhome, Luke, and Bryan things before, he said. I told him I was not interested. He said: "Don't knock it till you try it." I asked him to please leave and he did. After that I felt uncomfortable in Bryan's house. Bryan snuck in early that morning. I told him what happened. He thought it was funny, but I was pissed.

The Doctor asked: "Is Bryan gay?"

Daniel said: "I didn't know because I wasn't worried about it at the time."

"Why did he take you to an all-male club without warning you?" the Doctor wondered.

"He said it was about money," said Daniel.

He told me he had nothing, and this was a way to get what he wanted. He'd learned everything from Rhome and Luke. Poncho had raped Rhome, and Bryan thought Rhome had raped his brother, Luke. Thus the cycle of abuse started. Their little sister Becky became gay after Bryan slept with her. This was enough for me. I could not wait to go to AIT. Soon I was off to Fort Gordon, Georgia, but not before finding out that Bryan's little sister had been raped in a van by our cousin, Pharaoh. I took a cab to the bus stop and tried not to look back.

I had a great time at AIT. The first week there we were not allowed to have weekend liberty. The second week we all gathered with our battle buddies, getting a room for the weekend. We needed to release stress .I was infatuated with a girl from New York. I loved the way she talked, her attitude and her sex appeal. She was the only real dark-skinned girl I liked. She had a boyfriend who treated her like shit. I went to the PX with her one day as her battle buddy, and bought her a tennis bracelet for five hundred dollars. She said thank you and that was all. We never really spoke because we didn't want problems with her boyfriend.

She constantly had male friends, but I was too passive for an open relationship. The following week I met a girl who was a Mormon. She had never been touched before. I was her first. We snuck onto the parade field where we were forbidden, and I went inside her. Just as things were getting hot a light appeared. It was the on-duty sergeant. When he asked what we were doing, I said I was trying to get a nut, and I wouldn't stop until I finished. The girl was speechless.

We were escorted back to our units, and I took the blame for everything. When I saw her face again I regretted the entire incident. That night I was ordered to walk up three flights of stairs, pull everything out of my wall locker, and do ten pushups for each item. I did a lot of pushups until the sun came up. I stopped counting at about seven hundred, and was proud of myself. The following week I was promoted.

I excelled in school, as a communications specialist. A month had passed when I decided to go out again for the weekend. I met a new girl from New York. She was with her girlfriends also from New York. I got drunk as hell. I had a female battle buddy that I was not attracted to in any way, but she liked me very much. Yet she would not put out.

I went to the hotel where I had seen the white girl from New York. She had silver hair and a great black girl's body. I wanted her bad. She was surrounded by black guys who pretended to be ganstas. I let them, but when their loud music, childish behavior, and shit-talking got to me, I walked outside and she followed me. She said she wanted to stay the night with me. I didn't hesitate to take her back to where my female friend was. I took her in the bathroom. She said: "Don't kiss me, fuck me." I screwed her for hours, and came five times.

She couldn't take anymore. I did her on the wall in the bathroom. Cum dripped down her legs, onto the floor, and everywhere, I gave her everything I had. The shower curtain broke and we fell in the tub. When the sun came up we cuddled on the floor on the side of the bed; I was restless. I barely knew her, but there I was with the farts. The next night she slept with another guy, I couldn't understand how she could have done that after all I gave her, I hadn't thought she could handle any more.

I drank an entire bottle of vodka and went crazy outside. I kicked and screamed, actually having a tantrum. I tried to do some martial arts involving a brick wall. Standing in the middle of the street, I told the girl she was a fucking whore, and then I cried that I loved her. I went back to the hotel room and passed out for a minute outside the door. My battle buddy wouldn't let me in, and said she was going to call our command officer. I cried, kicking the door.

Eventually I called my mother. I cussed her out for not being there for me. She ignored me, then hung up, and I passed out again. When we returned to base the girl whom I'd bought the tennis bracelet, told me she had a crush on me, but couldn't date me because I'd slept with her best friend. After that I kept to myself until graduation, but I never forgot. That girl really did hurt me. It affected the way I looked at women. After all the years in detention, I didn't know how to start a serious relationship. It was a hard lesson, but how else do you learn except through experience or observation? Besides, I forgot all about my marble.

CHAPTER 19

After AIT graduation, I paced in front of the Columbus bus terminal for over an hour in a blizzard. It had been two days since I slept. My stomach had been rumbling the entire way. Twiddling my fingers in the pocket of my windbreaker, I pulled out seventy-five cents. It was all I had to remind me of my mother's love and expectations of me. Now I stood alone, teeth chattering, picking the lint from the three quarters, as I contemplated calling Bryan.

In the bus station I went to a payphone within view of my snow-covered bags. I was still cold but it was better than being out in that blizzard. Wiping the handset off, I deposited the first two quarters and held the receiver to my ear. "Please deposit another 25 cents," said the operator. With that I sadly deposited the last few grams of my pride.

The phone rang four times before he answered: "Yo, what's up?"

"Where the hell are you!" I shouted.

"Aw, I'm not here leave a message."

I had been talking to a voice recording. My heart sank—betrayed once again.

I walk back outside, retrieved my baggage, and brought it in. I made a little sitting area for myself. It was a depressing place. The few people there were probably homeless. I'd asked Bryan to pick me up at six o'clock. The clock on the wall said it was already eight. Twenty years old, and this is what my life had become.

I thought of walking seven miles to my aunt's house, but I didn't know if she still lived there. I was starting to think Bryan had let me down, I'd warned him and now he would have to pay for his treachery. I felt homeless, like so many other vets.

At 9am I wondered if he'd had a car accident. I grabbed my Japanese dagger out of the side of my suitcase. I overlooked the primary marble that lay beside it. I'd bought the dagger in Fort Gordon. Black leather lace elegantly accentuated the grip with the calligraphy "私の敵への死" (death to my enemies) etched along the blade. Holding the weapon under my shirt, I walked to the bathroom.

I washed my face, and looked in the mirror, contemplating the meaning of suffering and loss. I felt hungry, tired, fatherless and motherless.

My family had forgotten me. I reflected on the disabled with no limbs and little sanity. I recalled kids whose parents had actually died. Who was I to complain? Was my involuntary solitude a part of suffering?

It was my reliance on my mother and loved ones that had brought me to this point. *Why should they be allowed to walk with their heads held high?* I wondered. *They should pay for their inconsiderate actions.* I would start with Bryan. I slipped the dagger under my belt, turned around, and left the bathroom. I was adjusting the dagger when I looked up and saw Bryan in his white t-shirt and baggy jeans. Though he looked older, he still didn't have a care in the world.

"What's up cuzz," he said. "Sorry I'm late."

Saying nothing, I cautiously approached him and hugged him. With one arm around him, I grabbed my dagger with the other. The thought of penetrating him with the cold steel crossed my mind. His blood would warm the blade.

"I'm sorry," he repeated.

"Let's go, please," I responded.

By then Bryan had many girlfriends. He would take one girl's car and pick up another girl in it. He always appeared to have money. A lot of times he would leave me in strange places for the night. I got tired of that lifestyle. I tried to stay with my Aunt Brenda, but her son stole my money. I pulled a gun on him and threatened to kill him. His mom told us to leave. I didn't know why she kicked me out. I was trying to do the right thing. Later on I came to find out that her son was badly hooked on heroin.

I moved in with my cousin Stan, a black guy, who looked mixed. I think the Indian was strong in his blood. He was a 300-pound, 6-foot vegetarian who seemed to care about me. So many people had done him wrong that he didn't know who to trust. He was self-conscious about his weight, but refused to work out. I knew all he wanted was a girlfriend but it was hard for women to look past his weight to see his big heart. Bryan would try to sneak girls over there, saying Stan wouldn't mind. I refused to participate. Every time I stayed around Bryan my marble stayed yellow.

Everybody attempted to use me. I was pretty sure Stan had cameras in the house, and was always watching me. Bryan started hanging around more gay guys and stopped talking to me.

I would soon leave the National Guard and go on active duty in the Marines. I told Stan. He wasn't too happy about it, but thought it would be for the best. The National Guard wasn't happy either, but they said I had been a good soldier.

The Doctor said, "You went into the Marines to escape society?"

"Yes."

Bryan used my leaving as a gateway to get more girls. He would tell them: "My cousin is going overseas, and might never come back." It worked a couple of times.

Once at my Cousin Barbara's house, Bryan went outside and came back with two girls. I don't know how he did it. He took one of the girls upstairs. She was light-skinned, pretty, and had black hair down to her shoulders. Her friend was a lot darker with short hair that looked like it needed to be combed. When he and the light-skinned girl were done, he came downstairs and asked me if I had sex with her friend. I told him no. He then told me to tell her that I would give her $20 to give me oral sex. I told him that I couldn't. I'd never talked to her before, and it just felt wrong.

He said something to her, then went down to the basement. A few minutes later he came up the stairs and motioned for me to come down. I looked around the corner, and saw a pallet of blankets on the floor. She and I went to the basement. We got undressed. I still felt uneasy about the situation. As soon as she got undressed she asked me for the $20. I gave her a look of astonishment, then handed her $60. I couldn't get an erection, so I couldn't get the condom on. Instead I jacked off into a condom. Afterwards Bryan asked if we had sex. I said not really. I told him that I gave her $60 though.

He went back into the basement with my wallet. He opened it in front of her and said: "Put my cousin's money in the fucking wallet." He repeated it louder. She obeyed, grabbing the money from her underwear. I was amazed. I had never heard him sound this way before. Later he said I could've just given him the money, and he asked me for $35. I told him no. Later the girl apologized for even asking for the money in the first place. I told her that it was okay. She and her friend ended up staying for another five hours. This really bothered Bryan, so he eventually left both the girls there. I gave them $20 to get home; they looked like they really needed it. I wondered why a woman would sell herself. It lowered my opinion of women.

Bryan returned with Luke and we drank the night away. Finally Bryan took me to the airport, and saw me off. He told me how he envied me. He wished he could go. He said the family would respect me when I returned. I told him I doubted that. We waited for hours, and then, just like that, we said good-bye.

CHAPTER 20

I arrived at the airport in Charleston, South Carolina, with my marble in hand. We waited in a room for military personal only. A Marine came in, sharp as ever, and started roll call. The Marines were a lot stricter. He yelled for us to line up outside the room and not to look anywhere but straight ahead. "Nut to butt, nut to butt," he yelled, motioning for us to move tighter in line. It meant to put your balls on the guy's ass in front of you and your nose on the back of his head. I was so uncomfortable, that I had to put my mind somewhere else. I could have sworn I saw my mom out of my peripheral vision. This was possible. She was living in Charleston.

We got on the airplane and went to Parris Island. We were briefed on the way and were not allowed to talk to each other. Parris Island is just off the coast of South Carolina. As soon as the plane landed, the DI's (Drill Instructors) rushed us into formation. We were put into four squads and told to sound off. One, two, three and so on until every recruit was accounted for. Then the first squad would run onto the bus and the others would follow until the entire platoon was onboard. We didn't have to be told to be quiet on the bus; we just did it. They took us to the intake part of the base.

We were issued all of our gear and told to put everything we owned into a bag, including my fucking marble. If the Government didn't issue it, we didn't need it. They moved us so fast, always getting the right size shoes and equipment. We were assigned to our platoons. This was not the Army. We were not privates yet, we were recruits. There was no "Yes, Drill Sergeant," just, "Sir yes sir," or "Aye, sir." We were told to forget about everything we know or think we knew about life or the military.

Every platoon had three DI's. We had staff Sergeant Chukka, who was as big as a house. Also assigned to us were a Sergeant Perez, a short Hispanic, and Sergeant Thomas, 5'9", and 175 pounds of pure muscle. They all gave speeches. I knew that Staff Sergeant Chukka was going to play the soft role, the one you come to when you feel the DI'S were being too hard. I also knew the two Sergeants were going to run our asses into the ground. They made that clear when they told us to strip. The Doctor came in and examined us.

After the examination we did one last inventory of our belongings and changed into the uniforms we'd been issued. We had ten seconds, and we looked horrible. We did it again and again. Each time we failed to make the

time, we were dropped to do pushups; ten then fifteen, and then on up, till
I lost count. The DI's got louder and louder spitting in our face and
disrespecting entire family trees. They even talked about the religion on
your dog tags. I had put "none," so they told me the Marines would lead
me to heaven. It was hard for me not to laugh. I knew they were breaking
us down. After seeing DI Thomas strike a recruit in the mouth for not
keeping his arm straight with the M-16, it became easy to compose myself.
The DI's could not physically touch you, but they had a way of moving you
out of danger, so they put it, or correcting your actions, like grabbing the
M-16 and thrusting it until you hit yourself in the mouth.

The DI's also were allowed to protect themselves or others from
danger. So if you were in the pushup position or front leaning rest, he could
put his foot under your face. When you reached muscle failure and fell on
his foot he would kick your ass in self-defense.

*The Doctor smiled as if he knew exactly what Daniel was talking about. He had
heard this story before.*

Many times, as we lay in our bunks at the position of attention, others
would think about escaping, I would fantasize about Halisaseas. I didn't

know where it was but I knew it was better than here. It didn't matter. We were surrounded by water, and there was no escape.

If you didn't do as you were told you would get sent to a platoon that was a week behind yours. This meant you could do your entire four years as a recruit. You were pushed to go above and beyond your capabilities. Many nights we didn't sleep and many nights we cried. Some meals we didn't eat and some meals came out of the trash. I remember one day a recruit came to our platoon. He'd been sent a week back for not following instructions. It was our job as a platoon to get him through it. Every time he messed up we would have to do pushups. It wasn't uncommon for us to do a thousand to fifteen hundred pushups in one day. Sometimes the DI's would just smoke us, exercising us until someone vomited or passed out. The exercises changed very quickly, pushups, running in place, and mountain climbing. I knew this was to help us with our PT test, but many recruits did not. The Marine Corps was ninety percent mental and ten percent physical.

If you did not go to church on Sunday, then you had to stay and clean the bay floor with a toothbrush. I remembered going to church every Sunday. One time I withdrew my entire check and put it in the collection plate because I didn't need it, and thought I was surely going to die in the Marines. I hadn't realized I still had to buy shoe polish and military items that I'd lost in the field during training. They would promote and fire us all the time. They would blame innocent people then make us work out. I remember one day a guy was refusing to do pushups. The platoon had to do pushups until he got down on the floor. When he didn't, the DI stormed away and slammed the office door. I knew they were watching the entire time. We begged him to do the pushups, but he refused and cursed us. I lifted myself off the floor and punched him with a right hook, knocking him down then landing back on my chest. "He's down, sir," I yelled as the recruit started crying and doing the pushups. Another recruit from New York told him not to say a word. The DI's came out. They tried not to laugh as they told him to go clean up. They ordered us to recover or stand at attention. They then started parading around asking who the hell assaulted him. Nobody would say a word. Sergeant Perez took off his Smokey the Bear hat, and started poking people in the chest with it, demanding to know.   I stood out, saying: "This recruit did it, sir." I was willing to accept any consequences.

When innocent people are killed in a conflict they're called "casualties of war." I knew that I might have to do that eventually, but I was becoming reluctant. Admitting what I'd done to the recruit brought me one step closer to being a man, and leaving my childhood behavior behind. I had to take the consequences of all of my actions, even if this meant being dishonorably discharged and put in the brig.

The two sergeants dragged me to the head and punched me in my stomach, I couldn't help but smile as I hunched over in pain. When I came out the DI's said that I was the new platoon leader. I accepted this, though I knew I would pay for every mistake my platoon made. Two guys died during training and many got hurt. One guy jumped from the sixth floor, and another recruit from a different platoon stood up while taking live night fire. He crawled under the barbed wire, lifted his head and was struck by a tracing round.

Why did he lift his head? I don't know? Another guy went to the hospital after drinking too much water. They said his brain swelled. We never saw him again. Some said he died. As he lay in his bunk before they took him away, the last thing he called me was his angel. He said that I was bright as the sun. I felt bad for him, and wanted to give my marble, but I didn't have it. He was the one I had punched when I got promoted the first time. I became a strict and fair leader. By the end of that training I was used to people threatening me.

Every recruit must go through the Crucible, a test of physical, mental, and moral qualities. During this test we stayed a week in the woods. It was horrible. Before it was over we all had blisters and had pissed our pants. I was demoted from platoon leader, but they also called me a Marine for the first time. The demotion didn't bother me at all. I really didn't care if I led them across the parade deck for graduation.

My mother showed up for graduation, but there were no feelings between us. Marines are not allowed to show emotions in uniform. I didn't even hug her. I shook her hand.

Now there was nothing I couldn't do or take. After nine months in the army, and now the Marine Corps, I was ready for anything. All through boot camp I had been broken down. They'd literally pissed on me.

After basic I did not want to take a break. I went straight to Military Occupational Specialty (MOS) School, where I trained to be bulk fuel specialist. We had heard the news that there was an attack on the United States and that we were going to war. As I patiently waited for the order I was happy. A lot of people cried, but I was ready to kill. With my taste for blood, and so much hate in my heart, I knew I could not be a Christian. Nor could I be a Muslim. They put us on lockdown, and had formation calls many times a day. Military personal were not allowed to leave the base, and none but military were allowed on, but the war never came for us.

After school I stayed with my mom for month. I found out that she'd married a guy from Hawaii, Steven Googadan. He gave her everything. One day he told me he was in debt because my mother wanted so much. Though my marble hadn't warned me, I knew something was wrong with him. He was too nice. I could tell he was hiding something. Later I found out that he was connected with the mob. He did money laundering out of a car lot. When the F.B.I showed up, he was already gone. "Steven Googadan" wasn't even his real name. My mother had married a ghost. Even after he left, he stayed in touch with my mom, sending her money.

My next stop was Okinawa.

CHAPTER 21

My 18-hour flight to Okinawa was just what I needed. I arrived at the airport at three o'clock in the morning. They put me in first class. Our initial stop would be Hawaii. I had a bloody mary, but decided it was disgusting. From there I took a flight to Tokyo and the culture shock was amazing. I was on a small economy plane over the ocean. If a terrorist tried to highjack us, I was ready. Marines are always ready for war. I continuously watched my marble. I knew it would be my key to survival.

The first thing that stunned me was that they smoked in the airports overseas. They sold beer and cigarettes from vending machines. From Tokyo I flew to Okinawa, where I reported to my commanding officer. When I displayed my basic training attitude people smiled. They briefed us on the customs, laws, and regulations of Okinawa. For instance, if an American was driving, and had an accident, the American was automatically at fault. If one of us were to have sex with a Japanese college student who was a dependent of someone, we could be charged with rape. I had no problems adapting to these things.

I was fascinated by the tour we took around the island. They took us to island's caves and underground tunnels, and told us about the battle for Okinawa during World War II. It went on for three months, from April 1st to July 2nd, 1945. 7,373 Americans were killed, and about 32,000 were wounded. Our forces killed about 107,000 Japanese and we took 7,400 prisoners. Another 20,000 Japanese might have died. It was hard to tell because many were incinerated in the fighting. We stood on a hill the Marines had surrounded, and taken at great cost. Many Japanese took their own lives instead of surrendering. Some of the spent rounds still lay on the ground where I stood. I looked around and saw the statues and graves of the fallen. It was at that moment I bowed, and put my forehead on the ground. I felt so much pain there. I was impressed by the courage of the Japanese, but I couldn't help but think there must've been another way to resolve the conflict that ended so many lives.

Soon I found a special place there. I had to crawl through a hole four feet wide to get there, but then I could sit in solitude. It brought me to a room where the walls seemed to sparkle like diamonds, though I'm sure it was just salt deposits in the ground. You could see places where people had set up entire homes underground to keep away from the danger of the battle. That's how families protected themselves.

I recalled a scenario I was given during training. In this example I was supposed to think of myself as an officer in charge of extracting a family from a hostile village. I imagined myself, my team, and the family trapped inside a hut as the enemy closed in. When a baby girl begins to cry, I fear that our position will be compromised, so I order the mother to quiet her baby. She tries, but the baby won't stop. Now the mother starts crying. Tensions rise and everyone looks at me. Outside the enemy draws nearer. I snatch the baby, covering her mouth. I almost suffocate this innocent girl.

As her mother grows more hysterical, the baby keeps crying. I know that the approaching enemy will soon hear her, revealing our presence. Then everyone will be killed. If I were to survive, then they would torture me. What do I do? There was no right or wrong answer, but they said I would be liable for whatever decisions I made.   I thought to myself that no man should have life-or-death power over innocent people.

Every morning I saw Okinawans exercising. They moved gracefully, like tree limbs in the spring, swaying in a breeze. Occasionally you could hear a bong, which was the sound of meditation beginning.

In the field every marine was a rifleman. My MOS specialty was bulk fuel specialist. I was in charge of refueling aircraft, trucks and anything else that needed fuel. We had to learn how to set up refueling points anywhere in the world, air, ground, or amphibious. The new Marines did all the work, carrying heavy equipment everywhere. There was always something for you to do. If there wasn't, then you exercised. This went on from 5am to about 5pm. Sometimes we worked with civilian contractors who made more money than a Marine could ever dream of. I never understood why. These civilians could get us in trouble anytime just by telling on us. Even though we were the ones prepared to lose our lives, the military treated them better.

The Fleet Marine Corps was not the same as training. We still had standards, but we worked hard and played even harder. Marines would party at the local clubs all weekend. Some got in trouble for starting fights. I learned that the Japanese had a mafia, and they watched us all the time.

One of the first things I noticed in the fleet was the politics. Though education could earn you a promotion, it was also based on who you knew. Some of my MOS classmates were there. One girl, my friend, Garcia, shaved off all her hair after her stateside boyfriend broke up with her. I tried to comfort her. I even attended Mass with her. I wasn't sure what religion I wanted to join, but something was missing in my heart. I knew that the Catholics believed in Jesus Christ, and that he died for our sins. So I attended Mass with Garcia a couple times a day for a while.

I was the only black person there, but this did not discourage me. I even took the time to speak to one of the priests. He told me that I couldn't go to confession because I wasn't Catholic. I didn't understand this.

Shouldn't someone be able to ask for forgiveness whether he or she is a Catholic or not? This is when I really started to analyze religions. I noticed that the Catholic church was a huge cathedral, while the Christian church was held in a cafeteria. Soon I stopped going to church altogether. After I stopped, Garcia became antisocial, and stayed in her room.

I tried to look at religion from an outside perspective. I looked as Christianity, Catholicism, and Islam. None of them approved of worshiping Idols, and all believed in one only God. Most Christians believed that Muslims worshiped Muhammad, and they didn't think "Allah" was a name for God. I knew this was wrong. I knew that Islam meant submission to the will of God, and I learned that even Christians in the Middle East sometimes referred to God as "Allah." It was a part of their language.

Some people believed that Jehovah Witnesses worshiped Jehovah. They didn't know that Jehovah was another name for Jesus. People believed that Buddhists worshiped Buddha, but they do not. They follow Buddha's way of life, just as Christians do with Christ, and Muslims do with Muhammad. Some people believed that Catholics worship the Pope.

All the non-pagan religions have things in common. They strive for peace, happiness, love, and eternal life. God is love, peace, and happiness. Because the original language separated into many languages, he or she is known by many different names. Some Christians use the evergreen tree to remind themselves of the birth of Jesus. They decorate it with jewels and relics.

As of 2010 there were approximately 310,828,253 people in the US. About 76% of them celebrate Christmas by buying food, decorations, and presents. These transactions amount to $47,245,894,400, and average about $200 per person. Muslims would say that these people are spending too much money on a pagan belief, and that they are worshiping the tree. However, Muslims have Ramadan once a year. At the end of the fast many of them exchange gifts. The government and religious organizations reap financial benefits from these holidays.

I wondered how much the homeless benefit. Do they get 10%, or even 5%, of all that money? What good is a holiday plate compared to $47.2 billion divided among all the needy? The Muslims use a picture of the buildings of Mecca to remind them of a holy place. Isn't that somewhat like worshiping a building? Then there are the Jews, who call God: Yahweh. In Jerusalem they have their holy wall where they offer their prayers.

I began to think that all religions have some truth in them, but also that they are dividing the world. Satan uses this to conquer us. That made me think about the snake my friend had warned me about so long ago. It's our duty to seek the truth, and God is known to be the supreme truth. Religions are just as confusing as the languages that divide us. This is our test of faith.

I came to believe we should embrace all religions and strive for the common truth. After all, how could I shun something I know nothing about? I felt like this guy I knew in basic who said he'd never seen a black person before. There in basic, his DI was a black person. Up to then he'd thought black people were bad, even devils. He said that he was glad he joined the Marine Corps and found out the truth on his own. That brought me to a deeper thought: when we simply accept our parent's religion we miss out on so much truth in the world. Some religions try to keep their knowledge hidden to protect their way of life.

This was when I decided to abandon religion. Man had altered all the teachings in some way, so how could I find the original truth? With so many languages and dialects, how could one possibly find the original language? No one speaks it, writes it, or hears it. Even if we could, we would have to translate it, so it would lose some of its meaning.

Some Spanish words don't mean the same thing in English. Arabic words don't mean the same thing in English. One word from God that is misinterpreted could wind up meaning something completely different in English.

I had never realized that I could keep my faith, yet became lost again, and caught in a world of deceit. I'd heard all the theories about corrupt governments, secret agendas, and hidden religious organizations. People told stories about how revelations of these things could cripple the economy. I didn't know what to make of all that, but I knew I wasn't ready to handle it. So I walked away, mentally, physically, and spiritually.

The Doctor asked Daniel. "What did you do with that marble?"

"I put it up. I felt it had got me nowhere—just lost and confused. I also started to feel like there was no such place as Halisaseas, that we were all going to suffer, everyone in the world and what is the point of that?" Daniel responded sorrowfully.

CHAPTER 22

I didn't understand Garcia anymore. We were both devastated. Several nights I stayed with her in her room. We weren't allowed in the opposite sex's rooms, but nobody really cared. I convinced her to teach me how to dance. On many nights we would salsa together.

Weeks passed. She still wouldn't leave her room except for duty. She started to depress me, so I tried to find new friends. Soon I was dating a Japanese girl about 35 years old. She spoke little English. I was surprised because most of the Japanese on Okinawa seemed to speak several languages. After two nights we began to have sex. One night she snuck through the window into my room. She talked loud, and didn't much care for the government. She told me her father was in the mafia, and I began to suspect that she was a spy. Soon I decided that it was better to leave her alone.

I couldn't figure out why I couldn't have a regular relationship. I tried to date one girl who was in the military. She was not interested because I wasn't tall enough. Lots of girls wanted to be my friend, but that wasn't getting me laid, which was what I wanted. All I wanted was one girl who would have a real (and sexual) relationship with me.

Occasionally I paid for a five-dollar sucky-sucky, but that got old. I learned that Marines sometimes got beat up or killed off base when they were looking for that. I tried to find constructive things to do like martial arts. There were so many obstacles, especially women. Once again, I couldn't see the light. I started drinking heavily. Sometimes I woke up on the beach, or even in alleys. I thought God had abandoned me. I stayed in my room for as long as possible studying Hitler, Son Tu Zu (a famous Japanese general), and books on war tactics. I was shaping myself into an instrument of death. I slept under my bed, keeping my equipment, cleaned and accounted for, on top. I paid people to make me feel pain. I'd started doing this in the National Guard, but now it was different. Marines would hit me in the face and everywhere on my body. This was how I conditioned myself to ignore pain.

We spent a lot of money to make sure our uniforms were perfect, and the rest went to partying. When we'd been there for six months things started getting worse. Our superiors made inspections every day. If we didn't pass, they ordered us to carry everything we owned out to the parking lot where we had to clean it all—even our beds. Then we brought it back in for another inspection.

One morning, after a field day, we had a general inspection and my equipment was all polished and shined. The general complimented me on it. The rest of my unit failed, even the sergeant. After passing, I assumed I could leave my things the way they were, but when the sergeants did a follow-up inspection, they failed me for having my gear unsecured. It was on my bed, but they told me this was not a field inspection, so the rules were different. This pissed me off.

I was confined to the barracks, but I escaped out the window. Later, when the general came to the base for a drill ceremony, I snapped my M-16 barrel off. The general was impressed. He gave me an award, but the sergeant didn't let that go through. That's when I swore to myself that from then on I would only do the bare minimum.

One night we began a long exercise supporting a firefight against terrorists. In the darkness the trees became enemies. After days without sleep, we would look into the dark trees, and see figures moving. Four of us lost our rank for giving away positions.

When we'd been there nine months, we started preparing for Operation Iraqi Freedom. We were sent to an undisclosed island where we did not sleep for several days. After setting up camp, we were given weekend liberty on a nearby island. I remember like it was yesterday. It was nice.

When I found one of my officers in a local prostitute bar, he said: "Daniel do you know who I am?"

I was drunk, and had no idea at first. I just nodded "yes". Then it dawned on me: he was the chief warrant officer. I stared at the ring on his finger.

"You never saw me here," he said, giving me a look like death.

I got up and left the bar. I don't think I ever told anyone. That look of his scared the hell out of me. When I returned to camp I was put on mess duty. I wanted to kill, not cook. We spent two days in a huge cafeteria in the middle of the woods. Despite 109-degree heat I was not allowed to take breaks. I asked to take a break, but was denied because I didn't smoke cigarettes. You had to be a smoker to get a few minutes off.

When I asked the SSG for just a five-minute break to drink some water, I offered to screw in the poles holding up the huge tent on my return. He denied my request, saying he could shoot me if I didn't follow orders, because this was a time of war. I told him I had a rifle too.

He ordered me to start building a washroom for the dishes. The tent had to be separate from the mess hall because it had gas canisters and equipment. This was not my MOS. There was some equipment I wasn't trained to operate. I didn't want to get into any more trouble so I did as he said, but not before mumbling to him that I was going to blow this motherfucker up. I was excused from duty. A priest talked to me, but I didn't want to hear what he had to say. The next day I turned on a gas valve the way I'd been taught to, and then walked away. I heard an explosion. The next thing I remember is waking up in a chopper.

THIS PAGE LEFT INTENTIONALLY BLANK

CHAPTER 23

Daniel looked and at the Doctor, "So I suppose this is why I am here. Do I have a problem?" The Doctor told Daniel that he'd had a horrible childhood, and shouldn't be in the Marine Corps. "You've experienced enough," said the Doctor. "This is the end of our session. Go see the nurse, and I will get you out."

Daniel smiled and started back to the recreation room.

"Wait," said the Doctor. "I need that marble back."

Daniel reluctantly gave it to him.

The Doctor told Daniel, "If you stay on good behavior you can keep it." The Doctor explained that this meant not killing anyone, nor could he try to kill himself. Daniel promised he wouldn't.

As his time in the institution stretched on, Daniel began to get headaches. He lost track of time, and didn't see the Doctor for what seemed like months. He began to give up on life again and thought about killing himself. But finally they decided to send him to California to be honorably discharged.

Daniel still wanted to know if he had done a horrible thing. He wanted to know if he had a true mental problem. He figured that everyone had some kind of mental problem.

As Daniel got ready to leave the hospital, the Doctor told him he had a personality disorder. In Daniel's case that meant that he might react differently to similar situations at different times. This puzzled Daniel. After all, if someone were treated badly in the same way every day, wouldn't that person eventually change the way he or she reacted? Couldn't an attacker become passive, or a passive person turn into an attacker? Albert Einstein once described insanity as doing the same thing over and over, while always expecting a different result. So wasn't sanity doing something different instead?

Daniel had reached his breaking point, and it would take years for him to recover. On his flight back to Ohio he pondered all that had happened in the hospital. He knew he had big problems from his childhood, but if he was so hurt, how could he perform so well in the army? According to the

Marine Corps, he couldn't do any job. Daniel had never faced his past before. Now he wondered if he would ever make it to Halisaseas.

Daniel asked himself: "Why would they just release me into a world I know nothing about? How will I survive? I was once prepared to die for anybody who needed that, including my country. Did the government turn its back on me? Or did I turn my back on my country? Am I still a Marine? Am I a man? They told me at graduation: 'Once a Marine, always a Marine.' Most importantly: What did looking back teach me?"

* * *

Daniel's cousin Bryan ended up doing two terms in prison for raping and kidnapping two girls. Many of his friends and family members ended up in prison, some for life. Over the next several years Daniel continued his path, navigating through life's obstacles. He recalled his travels, and learned from his past experiences. He finally met a girl, and married her. She had brown eyes, and a caramel complexion. She accepted him for who he was, and for the man he was trying to become.

She knew Daniel was on a path to find peace. She understood that he'd spent his entire life running. Although she did not know the place he came from, she knew the place he sought. Daniel taught her to navigate through different perceptions. He told her to be on the lookout for serpents. She was a queen to him and the two of them made one. Many times Daniel would be provoked and it only took one touch from her soft hand to remind him of where he was, and what they were. She realized that Daniel had been unfamiliar with true love.

He seldom needed to turn to his marble for guidance. Life became an easier, more predictable road. He realized he'd traveled on it many times before. Though there were still occasional surprises, he had learned from his past.

Life was about learning and teaching others the undeniable truth. Daniel grew from experience and from observing others. Sometimes we cannot teach others through words, and must do it through our actions. We create the world we live in. In order to survive and cope, Daniel learned to balance his perceptions with the norms of society. His experience with corrections and the military was the basis for learning how to survive in a democracy. The U.S. Constitution guarantees us all opportunity. It was up to Daniel to find himself, and his place in life. He had the ability to do whatever he put his mind to, as long as his desires and actions didn't disrupt the system he lived in, "The American System."

Every one has a purpose in life. Daniel learned from experience and observation that doing drugs altered perception and prohibited one from travelling beyond one's means. Daniel liked Einstein's relativity theory. He understood that we are all connected. Inhibiting perceptions might be okay if a person wants to stay in the same place, but if someone is going to reach full potential they must be open to new perceptions.

Society fears what it doesn't understand. Daniel knew society, as a whole, was not ready to tap its full potential, but it was close. He often wondered where this would lead us a thousand years from now. Would free will be destroyed by impulse? The further he got in his thinking the less he needed a map. Daniel would become wise, knowledgeable and gain greater understanding of the world.

Much later Daniel and his wife stood on a Florida beach gazing out at the ocean. That's when he told her about the primary marble. He explained that he hadn't really needed it for years. She didn't believe Daniel until he pulled it out for her to see. All the primary colors swirled inside. She said it was the most beautiful thing she had ever seen.

Daniel explained to her that she was worth more than the marble. He told her about the many times he'd had reasons to die. Now he had many reasons to live. As he put the marble in the water, he glimpsed at his reflection. He smiled. He had found his Halisaseas. It had been within him the entire time.

Daniel had experienced shame, overcome lust and conquered his violent emotions. He experienced joy, becoming more optimistic. There was no dishonesty or cowardice in him. He'd mastered red. He had no fear of illness, because it was a part of enlightenment. He was no longer confused by hazardous warnings, He'd mastered yellow. Stability and peace had become a part of his life. He was loyal and was no longer depressed, He had mastered blue. His wisdom and spirituality became true.

You should visit Halisaseas sometime. It is beautiful, it is life, it is a part of you.

I remember meeting Daniel when he was a boy, telling him that everything would be okay. I am Aadil.

Authors Favorite Quotes

Booker T. Washington

Success is to be measured not so much by the position that one has reached in life as by the obstacles which he has overcome

Tully C. Knoles

The greatest thing about man is his ability to transcend himself, his ancestry and his environment and to become what he dreams of being.

Robert Heinlein

A generation which ignores history has no past and no future.

Jane Rubietta

Someone may have stolen your dream when it was young and fresh and you were innocent. Anger is natural. Grief is appropriate. Healing is mandatory. Restoration is possible.

Alden Nowlan

The day the child realizes that all adults are imperfect, he becomes an adolescent; the day he forgives them, he becomes an adult; the day he forgives himself, he becomes wise.

Harold J. Smith

More people would learn from their mistakes if they weren't so busy denying them.

M. Scott Peck

It is only because of problems that we grow mentally and spiritually.

Dali Lama

Share your knowledge. It's a way to achieve immortality.

Tao Te Ching

Knowing others is wisdom; knowing the self is enlightenment.

Carl Bard

Though no one can go back and make a brand new start, anyone can start from now and make a brand new ending.

Christopher Atkins

Now I'm growing and I can see my faults. I can look at myself objectively and say I can't blame anyone else; it was my own damn fault.

Socrates

The nearest way to glory is to strive to be what you wish to be thought to be.

William Spence

God,
Grant me the serenity;
To accept the things I cannot change;
The courage, to change the things I can;
And the wisdom, to know the difference.
Living one day at a time;
Enjoying one moment at a time;
Accepting hardships as the pathway to peace;
Taking, as He did, this sinful world
As it is, not as I would have it;
Trusting that He will make all things right
If I surrender to His Will;
So that I may be reasonably happy in this life
And supremely happy with Him
Forever and ever in the next.